TAKE YOUR MAT AND GO HOME

TAKE YOUR MAT AND GO HOME

a story of God's faithfulness

Blessings,
Maggy Allen

maggie allen

North Loop Books, Maitland, FL

Copyright © 2016 by Maggie Allen

North Loop Books
2301 Lucien Way #415
Maitland, FL 32751
407.339.4217
www.NorthLoopBooks.com

All rights reserved. No part of this publication may be reproduced, stored in a retrieval system, or transmitted, in any form or by any means, electronic, mechanical, photocopying, recording, or otherwise, without the prior written permission of the author.

Unless otherwise noted, all Scripture quotations are taken from The Holy Bible, New International Version.

ISBN-13: 978-1-63505-239-8
LCCN: 2016955532

Distributed by Itasca Books

Printed in the United States of America

CONTENTS

Foreword vii
Prologue ix

1. Room 908 1
2. Meanwhile, Jesus Slept 16
3. Take Your Mat and Go Home 33
4. Down the Path of Uncertainty 52
5. Washing the Mud from Our Eyes 71
6. The Promise of a Prayer 82
7. Abundance in a Den of Lions 96
8. The Ground Begins to Shake 110
9. Coming Home 122
10. Looking Up into the Light 140
11. This Is Not the End 161

Epilogue 180

About the Author 182
Acknowledgments 183

This book is dedicated to our daughter, Jesicah Ray Allen. Your name means "God is always with me", and I pray that you will discover that truth for yourself, not only within the pages of this book, but also in your own life's journey.

FOREWORD

For most people, life glides along each day with an occasional bump in the road. However, for Maggie and Josh Allen, a bump turned into a massive sinkhole when Josh's simple headache exploded into an eventual life-threatening diagnosis of Guillain-Barré syndrome.

This rare disorder would soon become a familiar enemy as it relentlessly and viciously attacked Josh's entire body for months with one horrific surge after another of pain, setbacks, and discouragement—physically, emotionally, and spiritually.

Maggie shares her journey with raw honesty on page after page of *Take Your Mat and Go Home* as she tries to make sense of a senseless situation and trust God to be her faithful Father.

I have known Maggie since she was born—a tiny bundle of bright blue eyes and a single strand of curly blonde hair on the top of her head. Combined with an ever-present smile, you have a clear physical picture of Maggie. I have watched her grow into a woman, wife, and mother who is deeply in love with her faith and family.

Then, I watched as her faith was beaten and battered by her husband's medical diagnosis, a situation that was beyond her human ability to withstand.

It has been said that if you "just have faith" everything will be fine. That's easy on the no-hassle days when all is well. But what about the gut-wrenching days when you watch the one you love more than life slowly slip away, and all the medical experts have no answers? Where is your faith then? And where is God?

This book is a must-read for anyone facing a crisis and feeling hopeless and helpless. Perhaps you're also struggling with your own bump in the road of life that has turned into a seemingly bottomless sinkhole.

Follow Maggie's journey as she encourages the reader to hold on to God's truth of his strength, love, and faithfulness. Discover how what we may see as an end is merely the beginning to God.

His words are simple: "Take your mat and go home."

Nancy E. Hughes
Author/Speaker
Lamar, Missouri

PROLOGUE

Summer 2013

Before July 2013, you could say that the life I had with my husband, Josh, was normal and predictable. Living in the Ozarks region of Southwest Missouri, Josh and I were blessed with stable jobs and a young daughter. In March of that year, we celebrated our ten-year wedding anniversary. In 2001, mutual friends introduced me to Josh, and we began dating shortly after. It didn't take long for his huge heart, sense of humor, and tenderness for his family to win me over. After our marriage in 2003, we spent the next few years building a solid foundation for our relationship by sharing some of our mutual interests like traveling, love for history, and spending time with family.

In January 2008, we welcomed our only daughter, Jesicah Ray, into the world. Fondly known in our family as Jesi Ray, she was a precious package of joy and smiles that would bloom into an entertaining, intelligent, imaginative young girl. Over the next five years, our lives remained on their predictable, sturdy tracks. Josh continued his employment with a truck-washing company contracted by UPS. His workload was a routine process of sweeping out the inside and power washing the outside of UPS package trucks and trailers each day. While there wasn't much variety in what he did, it afforded him a measure of consistency and reliability, and he had grown close to the people he worked with.

I had been employed for the past five years as a senior accountant for a local family-owned business that owns and operates franchise restaurants in various states in the US. I loved my job and the people I worked with. My accounting work was steady and dependable, as Josh's job was for him.

When Jesi was an infant, I began attending Glendale Christian Church with my best friend. In hopes of meeting new people and growing my faith through deeper study of the Bible, I joined a group of women that met once a week at the church. Through these studies over the next few years, I witnessed my faith increase and become strengthened. I grew to cherish these early morning meetings and the discussions that occurred.

Surrounded by friends and family living in our area, weekends were always busy and normally involved a large gathering of people and some form of barbeque. During the late summer and fall months, watching Arkansas Razorbacks college football was a requirement in our family. Lively game-day commentaries and friendly rivalries with Josh's cousins, who are passionate Alabama Crimson Tide fans, became an endless source of amusement and entertainment for us.

Another one of Josh's beloved pastimes was the challenge of a friendly, yet competitive, game of croquet. Rarely did we leave home without Josh's special mallet and lucky croquet ball; you never knew when or where a game could start up. When he wasn't watching football or playing croquet, Josh could be found sitting in his kayak with pole in hand, at one of his favorite river fishing spots. He lived for the great outdoors. It was his "happy place," his method of rest and relaxation from the stresses of life.

Our daughter, Jesi, was only weeks away from kindergarten and what she considered the greatest adventure of her life. It was all she could talk about. For the past three years, Josh had made a point of picking her up from daycare each day. Those afternoon hours before I came home from work developed into their special time together. They would take trips to the park, go for drives out in the country, and take our dogs for walks around our neighborhood. They had formed a special bond and become best friends.

Like I said: normal, predictable, and great.

Then the floor dropped out from beneath our feet. Our "normal" lives would never be the same.

Room 908 is where our story begins, but it is not where our story ends.

ONE

ROOM 908

"He alone stretches out the heavens and treads on the waves of the sea."

Job 9:8

I sat in stillness, listening to the soft humming sounds coming from the multiple pieces of equipment that were hooked up to my husband's intravenous drip. A few stray beams of light fought to invade the dimness in the room as the curtains shifted softly. Bright lights and loud noises were intolerable to my husband in his current condition. I tried my best to uphold his strict orders to keep the curtains closed at all times and converse with others only in hushed tones. I sat in the darkened room watching him sleep, my mind wandering back over the events of the past few days.

It had all begun with a simple headache two weeks prior. Josh was someone who rarely ever experienced headaches, and we originally concluded some form of allergies or sinus pressure might have caused the pain. However, as each day passed and the pain worsened, we both became increasingly concerned. Finally, we made the decision to take Josh to the nearest emergency room for evaluation. Blood tests were run, but the doctors were unable to determine the exact origins of the headaches, speculating that they might have been the side effects of a tick bite or virus.

Four hours later, we left with a prescription for both antibiotics and pain medicine. It wasn't safe for Josh to be driving at this point, so I offered to travel across town to the only twenty-four-hour pharmacy in our area. I spent the next hour waiting in line as patiently as I could, worry and fear clinching tight knots in my stomach. My hopes that the pain medicine would bring Josh some relief were short lived. The remainder of the night was a restless one for both of us. Josh found it difficult to sleep through the ever-increasing amounts of pain. Unable to lie down on his back, he tossed, turned, and eventually forced to sit up on the side of the bed in despair.

"The pain just won't go away. What are we going to do?" Josh mumbled, cradling his head in his hands.

"It's going to be okay. Let me go get another pain pill for you," I said.

I was running out of options, and comforting platitudes weren't what he needed from me at that moment. Grabbing his medicine and a fresh bottle of water, I sat down on the side of the bed next to him and wrapped my right arm around his back.

"I'll sit with you until the medicine kicks in," I reassured him.

"Thank you so much," he replied softly.

I woke up a few hours later to discover Josh wasn't in the bed next to me. It only took a minute to discover where he'd gone. I found him sitting in his chair in our upstairs family room, leaning back with his right hand raised up to shield his eyes from the sunlight streaming through the window.

"I can barely see, my head hurts so bad! What's happening?" The panic in Josh's voice was evident.

"Can you try walking down the stairs?" I asked.

"I can try, but I'm not sure I'll be able to," Josh said.

Holding his arms out and using the wall for balance, he slowly descended down toward our living room. It was then we discovered how weak his entire body had become. After an unsuccessful attempt to help him walk down the stairs, I realized that it was time to call Josh's parents and then 911. With trembling hands, I dialed my mother-in-law's phone number. They lived less than twenty miles from our house and I knew they could arrive soon.

"This is pretty serious, you need to come quick," I said to Josh's mom after she answered the phone.

While we waited for them to arrive and I listened to Josh moan in discomfort, I prayed. I prayed for healing, I prayed for rescue, I prayed for strength. I felt utterly helpless. I had never witnessed him suffer this amount of pain before. He was the strong and active one in our family. I was the one with a history of migraine headaches, and it was normally Josh comforting me as I battled through the pain. I grasped for sanity in these moments, which seemed to be swirling out of my control.

"Mommy, what's wrong with Daddy? Is he going to be okay?"

Our daughter, Jesi, had woken up and was aware that something wasn't right. I prayed that I wouldn't completely lose it as I provided only vague answers that I knew wouldn't satisfy her questions.

A sharp knock on the front door gave me the escape route I desperately needed, and I welcomed the two first responders into our home. As I watched the medical technicians attend to Josh, I had a strange feeling that I knew one of them, but I couldn't place how. Later, while we waited in the emergency room, I discovered that Daniel was an old friend from high school I used to work with at the local pizza parlor. I didn't recognize it at the time, but God had already begun reassuring us.

Leaving Jesi with Josh's parents, I rushed out the front door to follow behind the ambulance. The eight-mile trip across town to Cox Hospital gave me a few moments to be alone with my thoughts and have some deep conversations with God. I was in shock and I was scared. My brain was creating scenarios of what could happen, none of which had positive endings. Through a multitude of tears, I released all my fears and uncertainties, and turned them over to God. The peace and reassurance that were present with me in my car as I drove across town were less a product of my imagination and more the presence of the Holy Spirit.

The next few hours were spent in yet another emergency room, answering more questions and watching the nurses draw more blood. The attending doctor wanted to submit Josh to a spinal tap to rule out the possibility of bacterial meningitis. We were all relieved when the results came back negative. It was finally determined that the cerebral pain was due to a form of viral meningitis, but the doctor couldn't identify how Josh had contracted the virus.

God once again showed us signs of His unwavering faithfulness when we discovered one of the emergency room nurses was an old high school friend to Josh. Lacey stayed with him as the emergency room doctor administered the spinal tap to ensure that he was comfortable and to divert his attention away from the procedure. He was alert enough at that point to recognize her and briefly reminisce before the effects of the pain medicine prevented him from holding conversations. For a few brief moments, I breathed a sigh of relief. The doctor was hopeful that the virus would run its course and that within a few days Josh should be able to go home.

After several hours in the emergency room, Josh was admitted and assigned a private room. Our initial plan was for his parents to keep Jesi the next few days so that I could stay at the hospital with Josh. My parents had just arrived from out of town, and they offered to stay with me and keep me company while Josh rested.

It had only been a few hours, but already text messages and phone calls flooded in from friends and family members curious about the latest update on our situation. I felt extremely blessed to have so many people reaching out to surround Josh and me with love and support. It would be important for me to draw from these reserves of strength in the days to come.

Night would be descending upon us soon, and my parents needed to start their eighty-mile journey back home. I could feel exhaustion from the day's events begin to settle in as the initial shock wore off. I longed for a good stretch of my legs and a fresh cup of coffee. Not wishing to disturb Josh, I quietly made my way out of the room. After refilling my cup in the nearest break room, I walked slowly back down the hallway of the hospital's ninth floor.

As I approached Josh's room, my eyes drew themselves to the three numbers stenciled on the wall next to his door. Room 908. It was just a number, meant only for identification purposes, but over the next few weeks, this room would become significant as our story began to unfold.

Twenty-four hours after I had followed behind the ambulance to the hospital, I returned home, alone. My fingers fumbled with the keys as I unlocked the front door of our two-story house. I could hear the faint barking of our dogs, Jake and Isabel, drifting down from our upstairs bedroom. The door creaked open, and the noise of frantic barking grew louder. I took the stairs two at a time, released the hostages, and crumbled on the bedroom floor, opening my arms to the unconditional love that only dogs can provide.

Going back downstairs, I paused as the dogs burned off their unused energy in the backyard. The stillness of our house wasn't as therapeutic as I'd hoped it would be. Piles of dirty dishes were stacked in the sink. Clothes were strewn over the backs of chairs. Signs of hurried packing were brutal reminders of the previous day's events.

Overwhelmed with emotions, I closed my eyes and sank down on our living room sofa. I could still hear Josh's groans lingering in the air, the pain incredibly fresh. I struggled to fill my mind with the not-too-distant memories of joyous laughter as my husband and daughter played together. Everything inside of me hurt. With trembling hands, I lost myself in prayer. It was the only solace that would bring relief from the pain.

After a refreshing bath and change of clothes, I summoned enough strength to make the eight-mile trip back to the hospital. Deep pink and red hues with streaks of yellow in the sky demanded my attention as I walked across the parking lot to the front door. In that moment, I could feel God declaring His faithfulness to me once more. With head held high, I pressed the button on the elevator to the ninth floor.

Beeps and chirps greeted my ears while I headed down the hall toward my husband's room. Nurses spoke in hushed tones. I attempted to greet each one with a smile, even those who weren't attending to Josh. Taking a deep breath, I steeled myself and entered Josh's room.

Over the next few hours, insatiable bouts of pain from the meningitis assaulted Josh's head. The intensity of this pain would render him almost speechless and unable to hold intelligible conversations. Feeling completely helpless, the only comfort I could offer him was to cradle his head in my arms and hold him until the nurse came in with his next dose of pain medicine. Initially, this medicine was unable to last the full four hours required by the hospital between rounds, which made that last hour before the next dose the most intense for both of us.

That evening, after the relief from the most recent injection had begun to set in, I collapsed onto the small sofa bed while Josh drifted off into a medicated slumber. The tiniest amount of light or noise would bother him if he woke up, and he had firmly requested that I not open the curtains or turn on the television in the room, even at nighttime. I sat in silence, knees curled up next to my chest. I rested my chin on the back of the seat, staring out the window through a crack in the curtain.

I watched the world nine stories below me like a child who stares into a snow globe at Christmas. It seemed foreign to me, another universe. I silently imagined where the people in the cars driving by were traveling to and what their lives were like. What had only been a few days seemed like a lifetime. I felt isolated from reality. When Josh was awake, he was in pain and adamant that I remain by his side. When he was sleeping, I was so exhausted and overwhelmed by our situation that I could barely think straight. My phone vibrated and my Facebook account buzzed with multiple inquiries from friends and family curious about Josh's condition. I couldn't bring myself to respond. They would just have to wait.

Before realizing what was happening, tears began to stream again without reserve. I made my way to the small bathroom located just a few feet away and quietly closed the door. Greeted by the coolness of the tile, I crumbled to the floor, my legs no longer strong enough to hold me up. In that moment, every ounce of strength I had so desperately fought to maintain left my body in waves. I trembled as the force of my emotions overwhelmed me. I was scared and alone and I feared my world had just collapsed.

"Yahweh!" I cried out three times. I briefly lifted my head off the floor and threw my hands up in the air. Before the last syllable had left my lips, my prayers were answered.

"There you are, Lord," I whispered.

The first overwhelming sensation was indescribable warmth. It was the warmth of a mother's embrace, or a delightful spring afternoon. It was comfort and reassurance. The second sensation was an unexplainable peace. As the warmth saturated me, all the cares and worries of the world gently glided away. Left in its place was a confidence that despite the growing seriousness of the situation, we wouldn't have to travel this path alone. The third sensation of impossible joy approached as a soft whisper after the warmth and peace took over.

My tears began to dry and my body stabilized. With lips turned upward in a smile, I rested on my knees on the bathroom floor and worshipped God. For a brief, glorious moment, I found myself in the presence of Jesus and enveloped by the Holy Spirit.

Indescribable. Unexplainable. Impossible.

Only minutes before I felt my world collapsing around me, yet now my strength was revived. What happened to me was an amazing encounter with the love of God that met me in my darkest hour. He offered me a release from that darkness and provided me with another gentle reminder that I would never be left alone.

After my emotional encounter in Josh's bathroom, I found myself with an empty box of tissues and no one to talk to about what had just transpired. The remains of the joy were urging me to throw the door wide open, run to his bedside, and share this experience with my best friend. However, that wasn't possible when I closed the bathroom door behind me.

I was welcomed not with a smile and a curious grin, but with silence. A silence I was beginning to dread. Just moments before I had found myself swathed in the joy and peace of the Holy Spirit. Now reality reared its ugly face again and forced my emotional roller coaster to plummet back down the tracks. I walked over and stood next to Josh's bed for a brief minute, watching as he tossed and turned in his sleep. His face was the color of ash and there were large stress lines indented into his forehead as he fought against the pain, even in slumber. I patted the side of his arm gently, not daring to wake him up.

I sat down on the small pullout couch placed underneath the window in Josh's room, grateful for a place to rest. With a heart still racing and full of emotions, I knew that sleep would not come quickly tonight. Since Josh had requested that I leave all the lights as well as the television off, I had little in the form of entertainment to keep my mind busy. I pulled out the Kindle tablet I had packed before leaving the house earlier, turning on the night settings so it wouldn't disturb Josh. I opened up my Bible application to the book of Job.

Job lost his entire fortune and all his children in a matter of hours. It was a devastating blow. He had every right to raise his fist in the air and shout curses at God in frustration and anger. None would fault him. Instead, Job chose to react in a manner opposite of what anyone expected. Rather than rant and rave at the unfairness of his situation, he lay down prostrate in the dirt and praised the name of the Lord.

He chose worship over anger; praise over curse.

"At this, Job got up, tore his robe, and shaved his head. Then he fell to the ground in worship."

Job 1:20

Job raised his hand to shield the noonday sun from his eyes. He turned around from his survey to greet the servant who was running toward him, sweat beating down his forehead and lungs overworked with exertion from his mission. It took the servant a few minutes to catch his breath before relaying the distressing news to his master. Job's five hundred yoke of oxen and donkeys had just been stolen.

Before the last words had left the tongue of the first man, another messenger came running up to them from the fields where the sheep were grazing. Seven thousand sheep had just burned up in the field where they had been grazing, along with all the servants attending to them. Job could barely begin to process the news from the first two men when yet another servant approached them, agony etched into the creases of his forehead. Another raiding party had stolen three thousand of his camels and put to death all of the servants in charge of those camels.

Job's world began to sway like the branches of a tree during harsh winds. As he clung desperately to the tree trunk anchoring him to the ground, he received news that threatened to blow the entire tree down. Clutching his stomach, Job watched the servant's mouth form the words, but somehow they became suspended in the space between the two men for a few moments.

When the sound waves holding the message finally reached Job's ears, his legs buckled beneath him and he fell straight to the ground. All seven of his sons and all three of his daughters had been attending a feast held at his eldest son's house when a great wind swept in from the desert and collapsed the roof of the dwelling. None survived. It was all gone. His wealth. His property. His children.

Only Job, his wife, and the four servants grieving in the dirt alongside their master remained. Pain of this magnitude had never before shadowed his doorstep.

He glanced at the men in front of him as though he'd never seen them before. The grass in the field in front of him seemed frozen in time. Not a blade stirred. The immense weight of what had just happened floated in suspension directly above his head, waiting for its signal to be released on top of him. Job was afraid the pressure would be too much to bear.

In some of the darker moments during the past two days when self-pity threatened to take over, I had felt a similar burden of my own. My own tree, branches and all, had collapsed in shambles around me. Josh was my significant other, my better half, my best friend. I was overwhelmed, and like Job's servants, I struggled to catch my breath.

I felt the battle for understanding well up within my heart yet again. My husband lay fighting for his life on the hospital bed in front of me while Jesi was miles away from us, left worried and wondering about her daddy. What had happened here? What had we done wrong to deserve this? Was this some sort of cruel test? As Josh's condition worsened, I had more questions than I had answers.

I could not let the uncertainty consume me. For a few minutes, I laid the questions aside and focused on the praises in front of me. I suddenly found myself on my knees next to the sofa, lips moving in the darkness. I lay down in the dirt of my own circumstances—the uncertainty, the fear, and the anxiety—and left them there.

In that moment, while my heart lay open, God directed my thoughts back to that first day when I glanced up at Josh's room number in curiosity. I picked my tablet back up and spent the next few hours jotting down Bible scriptures, reading the stories that jumped off the pages below me.

"What are you trying to show me, God? How does any of this apply to what Josh and I are dealing with?" I whispered.

I received no immediate answer; no great revelation or lightning bolts from heaven. The room remained silent as I stared down at the tablet balanced on my knees.

"Have faith," my heart gently reminded me.

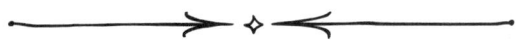

"You really should try to eat something." I said as I pushed the breakfast tray across the bed.

"It hurts so bad! I don't feel like eating right now!" Josh replied, turning his head to the side and away from the food in front of him.

This had become our new routine. Josh would sleep for a few hours, and then wake up as the pain medicine began to wear off. While he was awake, my presence was required to help soothe him as the next round of pain pulsated through his head. I would bend over the side of his bed holding his head in my arms, crying and praying with him. Both of us kept a close eye on the clock, anxious for his nurse to enter the room with the next dose.

I tried to reassure him that everything was going to be fine, the pain would end soon and he could go home in a few days, but I wasn't sure who I was actually trying to convince more. I had met his attending doctor just once since they moved Josh to his own room, and the only prognosis she provided was a minimum hospital stay of three to five days as the virus attacking his system ran its course. Until then, we simply had to wait and rely on the pain medicine for relief.

I breathed a sigh of relief when I saw his nurse appear in the doorway holding a syringe in her hand. Before administering the medicine, she paused to ask the obligatory questions regarding the level of pain he was experiencing.

"I'm sure you're tired of hearing this, but on a scale of one to ten, with ten being the worst, where would you say your pain is at?" She turned to look over at Josh while she inspected his IV drip.

"Ten! It's always a ten right now!" Josh exclaimed. I squeezed his shoulder as he covered his face with his hands.

Holding up her right hand in acknowledgment of his confession, the nurse finished injecting the dosage into the machine. Before leaving the room, she double-checked to see if either of us needed anything else, then silently closed the door behind her.

"What was the score of the Cubs game last night?" Josh asked. He glanced over at me and I could see the effect of the medicine begin to release some of the tension in his body.

I silently praised God for these rare moments when he seemed more like himself before he drifted back off to sleep. It felt like smiles were few and laughter even less between us these days. I tried to stay strong and positive for Josh, but I feared that my reserves would begin to run dry very soon. Occasionally, an aide or nurse who came in to check on vitals attempted to cheer us up with a simple smile or witty comment. These displays of kindness and gentleness from outsiders became a beacon of hope for both of us as we battled through this storm.

When Josh had fallen back asleep, I hastily finished off the uneaten cup of yogurt and washed it down with a now-cold cup of coffee. I sat back down in the chair next to his bed and stared at the blank screen of the television mounted on the wall across the room. I wondered how much more of this we would have to bear. What was this day going to bring?

Would it bring more heartache or more praise?

TWO

MEANWHILE, JESUS SLEPT

*"Suddenly, a furious storm came up on the lake,
so that the waves swept over the boat.
But Jesus was sleeping."*

Matthew 8:24

In the afternoon of the fourth day, I sat in the small waiting room of the hospital's radiology department, nervously shuffling through the pages of a *USA Today* supplement I wasn't really reading. I had chosen to wait downstairs while the technicians completed their procedure, rather than remain back in Josh's room by myself. This was their second attempt to retrieve a clean scan of his brain for analysis. The first one had been a complete failure the day before due to his inability to lie down flat because of the inflammation surrounding his brain. A clean scan would be very helpful for the doctors to determine why his body wasn't healing.

After more than an hour had passed, I checked in with the receptionist to see when he would be finished, only to be informed that Josh had been taken back up to his room some time ago after one more unsuccessful attempt. I thanked her and walked out into the hallway in a fog of frustration and tears. Traveling to the nearest elevator, I passed by hospital staff in the middle of their daily rounds and other patients walking the halls with family members at their side. Even though I was surrounded by people, I felt tremendously alone.

Upon my return to Josh's ninth-floor room, I found him resting once again. Quietly retrieving my cell phone, I left the room to answer a few missed phone calls and messages.

My heart soared when I saw the message that three of my Hamra coworkers would be bringing me lunch today from Pasta Express, one of my favorite Italian restaurants in town. I was thrilled at the prospect of enjoying a meal outside in the sun, even if for just a few minutes. I had initially requested to use vacation time until Josh went home, expecting to be out of the office for only a few days. I hadn't seen any of my coworkers since this situation began and I was anxious to fill them in on all the details.

I quietly left the room and walked down the long hallway to the elevator. I waited patiently for the elevator to descend toward the main floor below, knowing at the other end would be a few familiar faces. A warm July breeze met me as I exited through the automated doors located at the main entrance of the hospital. During the day, this area buzzed with activity; so very different from the hushed existence nine floors above. I was elated to see my friends, and I directed them to a set of picnic tables located in the shade.

"Why can't the doctors determine what's wrong with Josh?" one of them asked as we approached the tables.

"Have they given you any idea when he'll be able to go home?" another inquired.

"I don't know." I shrugged, wishing desperately I could give my friends some answers.

"How's everything going at the office?" I asked, picking up a breadstick and dipping it into the spaghetti sauce. As we chatted about work, I kept hidden away the late-night uncertainties of my own. Josh wasn't getting better, and the waiting and loneliness were unbearable at times. I braved the best smile I could muster and tried to enjoy the sunshine and fellowship, but I knew this brief reprieve would have to end soon.

"I promise to keep all of you informed with any updates," I said as we cleared the food containers and they prepared to go back to the office.

"If you need anything, please let us know." I embraced each of them once more, and then sat back down on the bench as I watched them walk away. A deep sense of loneliness and longing for normalcy overwhelmed me. My journey wouldn't be back to a workplace full of energy, but rather to a silent, dimly lit hospital room. For the second time in the same day, I felt tremendously alone.

That evening, Josh's best friend and his wife came to pay us a visit. Since he had been admitted, I had requested he receive no visitors, uncertain of how others who hadn't seen him for a few days would react to his current mental and physical state. This wasn't the Josh they were used to; the Josh they loved. The meningitis and pressure on his brain had reduced their best friend to a mere shell of a person. As my loneliness began to increase, I found myself making an exception to my own rule, in yet another desperate attempt to see a friendly face.

I was excited to see them enter the room, but immediately upset with myself as our friends took one look at my husband lying prone in his hospital bed. Their gasps and grimaces of shock spoke volumes. Josh was asleep and unaware of their presence, his right arm hooked up to various IV drips and machines monitoring his vital signs.

"I'm so sorry. I just can't believe this has happened, it's so hard to see Josh like this!" After a few more awkward words, they mumbled apologies, exchanged quick hugs, and left.

"Thanks for coming," I whispered to the door as it closed with a soundless hush. I wept in stillness, knowing that my friends' hearts were breaking, seeing Josh for the first time in this condition.

My worst fears were realized in allowing visitors, and the guilt overwhelmed me. My desire for a brief moment of normalcy had cost us all dearly. Anger swelled up, creating an unsettling tickle deep within my heart. It was pointless to be upset about our situation, yet it took every ounce of strength to fight back and prevent it from overtaking my soul.

I reached for my Bible and began reading a few passages in the book of Psalms, whose beautiful poetry was a balm for my aching heart. I couldn't control what was happening, but I could control my response. The promises held within the pages of the book in my lap were my only weapons against the hopelessness. I permitted the words to take root in my heart, declaring war on the enemy at my doorstep as I glanced over at Josh's sleeping form in the bed next to me.

I battled for understanding and wisdom. What was happening to Josh? Why wasn't the pain going away? Why was his body getting weaker? The fog of pain was much too thick. The ending of yet another day was upon us with more questions and fewer answers.

When my eyes began to close into a weary sleep, a picture formed in my mind and settled upon my heart. A lone figure stood in front of me with arms stretched wide. I could see the nail-pierced holes in his hands and puncture wounds in his forehead from the crown of thorns they forced him to wear. Reaching out toward me, I found myself wrapped in Jesus's glorious embrace. There was comfort in the promise that even though I might not understand what was happening, I trusted in the One who did.

The next day began the same as all the others. Soft light from the rising sun crept between the curtains in Josh's room. I shifted my weight back and forth on the sofa bed in one last attempt to get comfortable, but it was no use. Through the stillness of the room, I could hear activity in the hallway outside start to pick up pace. Morning shift change at the hospital was in full swing, which meant a new round of faces would be appearing in our room soon. My belly growled in anticipation of the breakfast tray that was sure to come.

Last night, the only interruption came from a laboratory technician who needed to draw a sample of Josh's blood. Josh had slept through this procedure, which I found unusual, but dismissed as the effect of the recent dose of pain medicine he had just been given. I let him continue to sleep as I prepared for the day and finished my prayers. A few minutes later, the kitchen staff delivered his morning food tray. He needed to eat before the nurses came in for their rounds.

"Josh, wake up. It's time to eat your breakfast." I gently nudged his shoulder in an effort to wake him up. After I received no response the first time, I attempted again to stir him from sleep by rubbing his arms as I spoke his name.

Keeping him awake, especially for meals, was becoming a major challenge. This morning I was less successful than usual. Even after I gently shook his shoulder and rubbed his arm, he could barely keep his eyes open and his speech slurred more than normal. A faint trickle of worry emerged from somewhere deep inside. The sudden appearance of Josh's nurse in the doorway interrupted my thoughts. She repeated my efforts to awaken Josh, with the same results.

"I'll be right back." The nurse looked up at me, concern clouding her dark eyes.

One minute later, she returned, declared Josh unresponsive, and initiated a trauma code. I heard faintly, as if through a dense fog, a voice on the intercom. The words to me at that time were unrecognizable.

"CAT Team STAT, Room 908."

The brief phrase repeated twice.

Within a matter of seconds, medical response teams converged upon Josh's room, hooking him up to machines and taking vitals while conversing in hushed, professional tones. I looked up at one point and made eye contact with Josh's mom, who had just arrived. The fear and panic I saw in her eyes was mirrored in mine. The nurses politely urged us to step into the small bathroom while the team attended to Josh. Under her breath, Josh's mom whispered an urgent heartfelt request.

"Pray."

"I am," I heard myself respond.

This was serious. The team was whisking my husband away to the Neuro-Trauma Intensive Care Unit many floors below. Standard hospital procedure required the chaplain on call to escort us downstairs. I felt a hand on my shoulder guiding me out into the hallway. With trembling hands and a shaking voice, I placed a call to our pastor's wife.

After the chaplain had directed us to the family waiting room adjacent to the ICU, we both spent the next few minutes on the phone alerting friends and family members. Only a few minutes later, my pastor's wife walked into the room with an energy bar and a warm cup of Starbucks coffee in her hand.

"I hope I chose the right type of coffee for you," she said after giving me a quick hug.

I was overwhelmed with gratitude at her response time and that of four additional church members deployed to the hospital immediately following my earlier phone call. They had just entered the room and agreed to stay with me until my parents, who once again had to make the hour-and-a-half drive across the state, arrived. I sat with the group in the large waiting room, staring at my cup of Starbucks coffee, listening to the upbeat and encouraging conversation flow. My smiles were genuine, but I could feel my heart slowly splintering into a thousand different pieces.

My thoughts wandered back over the past few days: the meningitis, the headache pain, the weakening of Josh's body, and finally, the weakening of his mind. I relayed to the group one of the more lighthearted stories from a few days ago. Each day, Josh's nurses would ask him a series of questions to evaluate his current mental capacities. One evening they asked him to state the name of the current president of the United States. Josh's immediate reply, without any hesitation, was "Will Ferrell"—the popular movie star. Snickering to myself, I watched the nurse question his response after giving me a curious look. With a hint of a smile, he glanced up at her and replied, "Well, he should be!"

This form of levity—the quick wit and even quicker smiles—was becoming a precious commodity in those rare moments where we witnessed glimpses of his former self. A wash of self-pity crept up slowly from the pit of my stomach as I thought of the things I missed the most. I hadn't seen Jesi but once in the past week and I missed her fiercely. I also missed my husband's physical presence, which at the current time was hooked up to an IV drip, heart rate monitor, and breathing machine.

With deep breaths, I fought back the waves of emotions and focused on the conversation at hand. My parents had just arrived and I said my good-byes to the group of visitors. After leaving my mom and dad with Josh's family who had gathered in a separate waiting area, I made my way alone to Josh's new living quarters in the intensive care unit. I pressed the large round button located on the wall that automatically opened the large set of double-doors. A sensation of medicated stillness permeated the entryway and spoke in intense volumes of urgency.

Josh's room was at the end of a very long hallway. To get there, I was required to pass by the other rooms first, each holding a single patient battling through some form of neurological trauma. I avoided eye contact with family members as I walked, silently praying for them. While privacy regulations prevented the medical staff from discussing each patient's diagnosis, I imagined they might be victims of stroke, paralysis, or car accidents. I felt an acute understanding of what those family members might be experiencing in that moment.

Finally, I reached the cube where Josh would be closely monitored over the next few days, steadying myself in preparation of what I would encounter. It was a long, narrow space with high ceilings, large enough to hold his bed, a small sink, and a few chairs for family members to use. A few windows had been set close to the ceilings in the wall behind the bed to allow a small amount of light in. What took my breath away, however, was not the contents of the room, but what I saw when I walked through the door.

The form lying on the bed was still, his face covered by a mask connected to the breathing machine chirping on the stand next to him. My knees went weak and I feared they might buckle. Along with the weakening of Josh's body and mind, his lungs were now compromised. In his current position they were unable to sustain normal breathing patterns on their own, and the use of a machine to help regulate his oxygen input was required.

Unable to breathe on his own.

Unable to retain clarity of mind.

His life hung in the balance.

I had witnessed him stand up only twice in the past week. The last time I had seen him sit upright in a chair was two days ago. His doctors had requested that I try to get him out of bed and sit up for a few hours, both for his physical and mental well-being. It had taken one of the nursing aides and myself several minutes to navigate him from his bed and over just a few feet to the chair. By that point, his body had become so incapacitated by the pain medicine that the use of a pillow to support his head was required, and he was unable to stay awake for very long.

I sank down into the overstuffed chair provided for family members and watched the numbers on the breathing machine rise and fall. My mind felt numb. Rain began to fall in earnest outside the small window located above his bed. I attempted to pray, but my train of thoughts became incompetent babble. As traumatic as the past few days had been, I felt an even greater intensity begin to build. What would transpire tomorrow, or even within the next few hours, I couldn't imagine. I was left without words.

Only God knew. Only He could provide us with the strength to endure.

Later that evening I returned once more to our empty house across town. Due to the severity of this latest turn of events, I had made the decision to keep Jesi away from the hospital and remain with Josh's parents until his condition had improved. It was emotionally devastating to be separated from her for such a long period, but with all my energy directed toward Josh, I simply didn't possess the strength to take care of anyone else.

I traveled up the stairs to the bathroom in a fog of exhaustion and drew a fresh bath with water as hot as I could handle. Our claw-foot bathtub had recently become my personal safe haven. It was the only place in the world where I was left completely alone; with myself and with the emotions of our situation. In this space, I allowed myself a welcome invitation for release. Once a day, I let go of everything. I prayed. I screamed. I whispered. I held myself and rocked back and forth as wave after wave of pain coursed through my soul.

Just like my previous experience in Josh's bathroom in Room 908, I'd cry out and the Holy Spirit would appear. It always began with a warm internal glow followed by a peace that could calm the fiercest of storms. There was no need for dramatic openings in the sky with angels singing "Hallelujah!" I simply knew He was there.

Before heading back to the hospital, I chose to take a few quiet moments for myself. Resting on the couch in our living room with a dog lying on either side of me, I picked up my Bible and turned to the book of Matthew. As I read the story of Jesus calming the storm, I felt a trace of reprimand regarding my earlier display of disbelief. Where was my faith, exactly? How many times would I have to let this lesson repeat itself before I could allow myself to fully trust in the promises God made me? Did I really believe that He was thoughtlessly unaware of what was happening and would abandon us in our time of need?

I had acted just like one of the disciples, begging Jesus to wake up and calm the storm, only to lose sight of the fact that it was Jesus who had control of the storm all along. I didn't need to be afraid. My boat wasn't going to sink.

> *"He replied, 'You of little faith, why are you so afraid?' Then he got up and rebuked the winds and the waves, and it was completely calm."*
>
> *Matthew 8:26*

The night was clear, with only a scattering of clouds in the west as the disciples followed Jesus on to the boat. Setting sail on the Sea of Galilee, the waters beneath them were calm and the boat rocked gently back and forth. The group rested comfortably and conversed in hushed, excited tones about the events of the day while their teacher slept peacefully in the corner of the boat. With their attentions fixed on a particularly animated retelling of a story by the brothers James and John, none of them noticed the billowing clouds filled with rain and lightning that formed on the horizon.

The disciples were caught by surprise as fierce winds began to swirl the sails of their boat and the swelling of the waves underneath rocked them back and forth in violent motions. The men raced around in desperation around the boat, securing the sails and ensuring that no cargo or supplies found their way into the water. Fearful of what might happen to their primary source of income, they rushed over to Jesus for guidance.

Except Jesus was sleeping.

Imagine their surprise to see their Master sleeping like a baby while this fierce storm raged all around them. Awakened by the cries for help, Jesus stood up and reprimanded his followers.

"O ye of little faith!"

With one wave of his hand, the wind stilled and the waves calmed. The raging and blustering storm that had only seconds before threatened their very lives was now banished. Even though the disciples understood with whom they sailed, they still fretted and worried about how this particular day would end. In doing so, they displayed a lack of faith that Jesus would not be able to provide for their safety and their needs.

Walking through the doors of the hospital one hour later, my soul felt rejuvenated. Nothing had changed. Josh hadn't been miraculously healed and our situation was just as dire as before. What had altered, however, was something inside of me. I wasn't the same person I had been only a few days prior. My faith had been stretched to points beyond comprehension. At times, I feared that I would not be strong enough to make it through this, that I would crumble beneath the weight of fear and uncertainty. What began to shift within me was the realization that I would never have enough strength to endure, not on my own; and that was okay. Jesus would provide for me.

The next few days were filled with lots of rain and even more silence. The hushed volume of the intensive care unit fostered reflection and compassion as each patient surrounding Josh dealt with various levels of trauma. Josh himself had yet to make a full recovery back to a state of wakefulness, only being alert long enough for the nurses to take his vitals and make attempts at eating.

Those efforts resulted only in failure because the muscles in his body were so weak. He wasn't able to grasp and hold on to eating utensils. I began to sense the medical team's frustration at his inability to feed himself. They had discouraged me from helping him, believing that his lack of desire to pick up food from the table in front of him was actually a sign of laziness, not weakness. The nurses finally decided that feeding him liquid supplements through a straw was the only option. Josh's physical therapists continued to make their daily rounds, hoping that they could help him regain some of the motor skills he was rapidly losing.

Josh now had a whole team of doctors working diligently around the clock to rule out every possible diagnosis: neurologists, oncologists, and an infectious disease expert. With the exception of the original meningitis, all their tests came back negative. The very sight of this team descending upon his cube caused my heart rate to spike. Unsure of what their newest update would bring, I couldn't determine whether the news would be hopeful or discouraging.

Today's update would include one more request for a brain scan in hopes that it would be more useful to the doctors than the last few. A clean scan would be vital for a correct diagnosis. They assured us that while Josh wasn't going to be completely sedated, he would be given an appropriate amount of medicine to relax his muscles and make him feel more comfortable. Comfortable wasn't a word I would use to describe how I felt about this. It would be the same procedure that had caused undue stress twice before.

Watching the nurses wheel his bed out of the room, I sank down into the nearest chair. Fat drops of rain continued to blanket the world outside and for a few minutes, they were the only activity that held my attention. Once my interest in the rain faded, I turned back to my notes taken during the first few days of Josh's hospitalization. I had a list of seventeen Bible verses that I kept with me at all times. Reflecting on one of those scriptures each day had become part of my routine.

I opened my Bible to the book of Numbers. Reading in silence, I contemplated what it would mean to trust implicitly and unconditionally in a plan where I had no knowledge of what was going to happen—as Abraham experienced when God instructed him to sacrifice his only son. Like Abraham, I sensed that God was encouraging me to remain faithful, despite the unknowns of our current circumstance. Even if waters of fear and uncertainty surrounded us, he promised the rain wouldn't last forever and the sun would one day return.

> *"In other words, it is not the children by physical descent who are God's children, but it is the children of the promise who are regarded as Abraham's offspring."*
>
> *Romans 9:8*

His hands trembled as his wife handed over the small bundle for him to hold. The baby had just eaten and was now sleeping. Sarah watched Abraham's face as he cradled the infant in his strong arms. A mixture of joy, amazement, and contentment passed over him while he watched his son sleep. It was a miracle that Isaac was conceived; a miracle that Sarah had survived the struggle and pain of bearing a child. God had kept his promise.

Many years earlier, because of Abraham's faith and obedience, God had promised him that his descendants would number more than the stars in the sky. He was to become the father of the Israelites. There was only one problem with that declaration. His wife, Sarah, was barren. It seemed impossible to him that one day he would have descendants too numerous to count.

Yet, Abraham still believed. He held closely to his faith because time after time, God had proven faithful to him. Even when he approached the age in his life where childbirth would be close to impossible, if not life threatening for his wife, his faith did not waver. He believed that God's timing was perfect and Abraham trusted in His word.

And then the unimaginable occurred. When Sarah reached her nineties and Abraham was one hundred years old, Sarah became pregnant with a son. They rejoiced and praised God together when Isaac was safely delivered into the world. She had laughed at the suggestion that she would be able to give birth at her age, but now the laughter filling their household was from the joy they both felt. God was faithful.

The proud parents watched as their infant became a toddler, learning to talk, walk, and engage with the world around him. In what seemed like the blink of an eye they witnessed their growing son become a young man. It was then God called Abraham to be obedient once more.

Abraham was requested to do something that few of us could even contemplate. The Lord wanted him to take Isaac, his beloved son, and offer him as a sacrifice. The next morning, he prepared for the trip and gathered Isaac, two of his servants, and his donkey. It took a heart full of the greatest obedience and trust in God to make the journey up that mountain.

When the group had reached their final destination, Abraham began preparing for the sacrifice. He still didn't know how he would be able to complete the task, but he continued to have faith. Then, at the very last moment, God made a surprise play. He provided a ram caught in the bushes nearby as a replacement for the sacrifice, instead of Isaac. God had asked Abraham to do the unimaginable, and instead of questioning or complaining, he had laid aside his emotions and obeyed. He had faith that God knew exactly what He was doing.

Sitting my Bible down in my lap, I closed my eyes, cleared away all the uncertainties rattling around in my brain, and reflected on the promises of God. This redirection of my thoughts brought with it a renewed sense of encouragement and understanding. The answers I was seeking—why this was happening, what the future would hold for our family—would be revealed to us in His time. All that was requested of me this day was to be faithful.

THREE

TAKE YOUR MAT AND GO HOME

"When the crowd saw this, they were filled with awe; and they praised God, who had given such authority to man."

Matthew 9:8

Josh had now been in the hospital for seventeen days. After several days of stabilized functions, the doctors determined that he was now able to move out of intensive care and back up eight floors to the wing of the hospital specifically dedicated to patients with neurological conditions. Our family rejoiced at this small victory even though Josh's overall condition remained the same. The use of the breathing machine was still vital while he was sleeping, and he was rarely awake for any length of time.

We fought daily against frustration with the hospital staff at various levels. The revolving door of nurses at every shift change became for us a revolving door of emotions. We praised those who had exceptional bedside manners and compassion and suffered through those who seemed to lack proper etiquette or training. During the days on the ninth floor, there were times when I had to walk down to the nurse's station because no one responded to his call button. It seemed as if everyone had an opinion on Josh's condition, yet no one could provide us with solid answers.

Josh's care routine had changed dramatically with this recent move, and we continued to pray for wisdom and guidance for those responsible for him. He was beginning to develop a bedsore and his nurses were instructed to reposition his body every few hours to keep the sore from growing. He couldn't sit up by himself, nor move from his bed to his chair. The only way to move him around the room was with the use of an electronic lift; a procedure we soon discovered lacked training on the part of some nurses and aides. Despite those frustrations, the special care for Josh and compassion for our family displayed by other hospital employees was a blessing not taken for granted.

I had been absent from my accounting job at Hamra for several weeks. All the sick and vacation time available to me was gone, and I now needed to prepare my heart for a return to work. I began to battle against a new form of anxiety. It whispered thoughts and fears that wrapped silently around my heart. I had lost my "normal" life. What would become of our finances with Josh unable to work? How could I go back to work and pretend everything was fine, when it really wasn't?

This particular nemesis desired to leave me with only questions; threatening to consume me and paralyze my faith into a constant state of dread. I knew that it was going to take an additional amount of supernatural strength to rid myself of this vicious adversary.

As the sun rose the following day, banishing the rain that had plagued us for so many days, filtered beams of light shone through my bedroom window. I glanced over at my sleeping daughter. Tears welled up as I brushed a wayward strand of hair away from her eyes. Only days away from her first day of kindergarten, her innocent and carefree life had been brutally interrupted, yet she was still able to produce a smile when she awoke to the sound of my voice. Wrapping my arms around her, I prayed for the strength to be strong for this little one, to bear the weight of what this day might bring, for the simple fact that she needed me.

Today was my first day returning to work, which meant that I no longer spent the night at the hospital with Josh. Jesi was thrilled to be back home and to have more time alone with me. After getting ready, I dropped her off at daycare and made the now-routine trip to the hospital. I had arranged with my supervisor to spend a few hours each morning with Josh before going to the office. This enabled me to continue supporting my husband while still maintaining the normal responsibilities of my job. Taking a deep breath before exiting the elevator, I quietly centered on my "one day at a time" perspective. I found the constant repetition of this short phrase therapeutic and it forced my mind to focus on the most important fact—the future was not mine to control.

A few days ago, a suggestion made in passing by the attending nurse about giving Josh a foot massage had sparked my curiosity. I was interested in trying it out today. Poking my head around the curtain in Josh's room, I was overjoyed to find him awake, the remains of breakfast left on his tray. With a crooked smile he glanced up at me, warmth radiating from his green eyes. I immediately located the bottle of cream the nurse had given us and began to massage his feet and ankles.

"How does that feel?" I asked Josh while I continued rubbing his left foot. The side effects of lying in a hospital bed for seventeen straight days had taken its toll on his body. His legs and feet were in desperate need of positive blood flow. The nurse had suggested the massage in hopes that it might help stimulate his blood vessels and possibly energize the nerves in his feet enough so that he could begin to walk again.

"I can't feel anything." Concern clouded Josh's face as he responded to my question. I switched over to massage his right foot and lower leg next, testing his response at various levels of pressure.

"Anything now?" I tried to keep my voice from trembling as I glanced up at him from the end of his bed.

"Nothing," Josh replied in frustration.

Our discourse was interrupted by the surprise appearance of four doctors with gleaming white coats in the doorway of Josh's room. The team consisted of two lead doctors along with two medical students trailing behind them during their morning rounds. The most senior doctor took a step toward me as I stood up to greet them.

"We need to run more tests," he said, without a trace of emotion in his voice.

"Of course, I understand." I nodded my head toward him, holding back another round of tears.

One more day without answers. I watched them turn around and exit the room as quickly and quietly as they had entered. Taking several deep breaths to steady my nerves, I returned to the chair I had pulled up next to Josh's bed, not wishing him to witness how unsettling their words had been to me. I was relieved to see that he had fallen back asleep and was blissfully unaware of the doctor's conversation.

Leaving Josh to his rest, I took a few minutes to check in on e-mails and messages I'd received that morning. Responding to daily inquiries from friends and family was at times both emotionally relieving and draining. I desperately desired to give them the answers they sought—that we'd finally received a diagnosis, that Josh was going to come home soon, and that everything was going to be fine. Unfortunately, I could deliver none of these today.

My heart rejoiced to see a message that one of Josh's friends would be visiting him today. Our family had kept visitors mostly at bay while he was in intensive care due to their stricter schedules and the simple fact that his current mental and physical condition wasn't conducive to company. He was slowly beginning to come out of the mental fog that had held his mind prisoner for so long and we began encouraging visitors to come to the hospital and see him. I prayed for every encounter he had with the outside world, hoping they would provide the sparks needed to bring him back to us.

When blue skies and bright sunlight filled the room, my thoughts wandered toward what our life would appear like after this rainstorm. The events of the past few weeks had brought with them a personal reassurance from God, in many different forms, that we would not weather this storm alone. As this solid foundation was laid underneath our feet, I became more intrigued about how God was going to use our story as part of His greater plan.

Standing at Josh's window, I watched as cars drove by and visitors entered the hospital eight floors below, oblivious to what we were going through. Was I oblivious to what was actually happening in this hospital room? Closing my eyes, I prayed less for answers to my questions and more for wisdom to see the glory of God revealed.

After my prayers were completed, I opened up my Bible to the scripture in the book of Matthew I had chosen to reflect on today. A prickly sensation overwhelmed me as I read the story. I remembered writing it down on paper while chuckling to myself, wondering how the story of a lame man could apply to Josh. I glanced up from the text over to the lame man who lay on the hospital bed in front of me, in awe. The path had been laid down before me. All along, God was gently placing reminders of His faithfulness in my life.

I only had to open my eyes wide enough to see them.

*"So he said to the paralyzed man,
'Get up, take your mat and go home.'"*

Matthew 9:6

Down a dusty road littered with animal droppings and hollows where rain had washed the packed earth away, two lone figures struggled to balance the weight of the mat that carried their friend. They had heard rumors about the mysterious stranger who was traveling through the countryside performing miracles and healing the sick. No doubts passed between them as they weighed the options. They simply picked up their friend, who was unable to stand up on his own, and carried him to meet this miraculous healer.

With anxious and hopeful hearts, they approached the crowd that began to materialize as news of Jesus's arrival quickly spread across town. Arms trembling, they navigated through the mass of people, desperate to locate a spot close to the healer. To their dismay, they discovered the large gathering was actually overflow from the entryway to a house where Jesus was teaching. They were too late. At this point, there was no feasible way inside and through the throngs of people.

With jaws set in determination, they were determined not to leave this place without seeing this famous healer in person. One of the men noticed a ladder leaning up against the side of the house. Apologizing to their lame friend for the uncomfortableness of the situation, the stronger of the two offered to make his way up the ladder carrying the paralyzed man on his back. More people met them when they reached the rooftop; however, the crowd was not quite as thick and they were able to maneuver toward the opening to the lower floors below.

And then, there he was. A small clearing was made in the room for Jesus and his disciples. Locking eyes, the friends nodded to each other in agreement of their next course of action. They each grabbed pieces of rope that had been lying in a pile over in the corner of the rooftop and secured them to the ends of the mat. The other men on the roof next to them shook their heads in disbelief as they realized what the friends had intended. After verifying the ropes were secure, they slowly began to lower their lame friend down through the opening.

The crowd buzzed with curiosity as they watched a strange man being lowered down directly in front of where Jesus was standing. Raising his hand in a polite request for the others in the room to be silent, Jesus bent down next to the lame man with an affectionate smile on his face and rested a hand on his shoulder. The man lying on the floor felt an unexpected sensation of peace surround him.

"Take heart, son; your sins are forgiven.

Get up, take your mat, and go home."

Slowly, as if in a dream, their friend began to rise up from the ground. Both men looked at each other in amazement, then back down through the opening to the man who had spoken the words. They had journeyed down this hopeful path, not certain of what to expect. Now they would be walking back beside their friend, carrying his own mat home.

I read over this story multiple times, and with each reading discovered something new. These men were not followers of Jesus who had seen him perform numerous miracles, they had only heard of these things in passing. Yet they still had enough faith to pick up their lame friend and carry him several miles to the place where Jesus was teaching. I can only imagine the sheer joy and amazement they felt when they saw their friend stand up from the floor and walk out of the house on his own two legs. I can see the loving smile on Jesus's face as he watched the three friends reunited, embracing each other in exuberance.

Faith in what they could not see, and daring to hope, led those days. Similar to their faith, it would only be through hope in what I could not imagine that would bring a smile to Jesus's face, as he reached his hand down to pick us up from the dirt.

Later that morning, I was overjoyed when Josh's therapists recommended taking advantage of the recent shift in weather and have him sit outside in his wheelchair for a few minutes. While Josh had been in intensive care, these same therapists tried several times to get him to stand up and walk, with little success. Now realizing the weakness of his lower body prohibited such efforts, their focus shifted to simply getting him up and out of bed.

The task seemed easy enough. It took twenty anxious minutes, however, to maneuver my six-foot-tall husband from his bed over to his wheelchair using an electronic sling and pulley system. My heart lurched at the sight of him upright, sitting in his chair. He hadn't been out of his bed in a week, and as I followed behind the therapists down the hallway, I understood the importance of this small victory. Maneuvering the wheelchair into the elevator, the younger therapist leaned over as he patted Josh on the shoulder, speaking quietly under his breath.

"My family and I have been praying for you each day at dinnertime," he said, with concern in his eyes.

"Thank you so much," I quietly responded.

Josh's mysterious condition wasn't only concerning to his doctors, but also to those within his circle of care. This young man understood that Josh had entered the hospital able to use his legs, but now faced the possibility that he might not go home that way. He'd gone beyond his clinical duties in extending compassion toward Josh and me. It was a refreshing sentiment in a world surrounded by anxiety and uncertainty.

I followed the therapists through the double doors of the main entrance to a concrete bench located only a few feet away. After confirming that Josh's chair was locked into position, they went back inside and left us alone. The warm sun proved too overwhelming for Josh, who began to weave in and out of consciousness. I decided to join him and closed my eyes for a minute while I listened to the gentle gushing sounds of the water fountain nearby.

I used these precious minutes to clear my head and reflect on the blessings that continued to flow into our lives. I marveled at how many people around us were lifting us up in prayer every day. It truly felt like we had our own army of prayer warriors petitioning our situation before the Most High. Even in that very moment, I could feel the peace from their prayers surrounding and encouraging me.

I thought back over the day before when Josh's best friend, who had known him since high school, stopped by the hospital to deliver lunch for me. Choosing to meet him in the hallway rather than disturb Josh, we chatted briefly about the most recent medical updates. Eyes glistening, he relayed a conversation he recently had with another high school friend who mentioned that he had begun to pray for Josh. I was surprised to hear of prayers offered to God from people who might not seem from outward appearances to be extremely religious. I noticed the humility in my friend's eyes as he admitted his own need to draw closer to God these past few weeks.

My heart soared with encouragement to visibly witness God at work, not only in our own lives, but also in the lives of those around us. I had prayed for wisdom to discern how our situation would be used, and God answered. It was a revival of sorts; a return to what was truly important. As in many traumatic medical situations, there was a universal heart-cry of compassion and empathy for Josh and me that broke through religious barriers. I could feel a shift in my own faith and in the conversations that were taking place. I began to point less at the circumstances and more at the One who had the solution. Through my heartache and weariness, hearts were softened and the possibilities of a source of power greater than our own were explored with each prayer.

I was certain that even the least of God's plans would be more amazing than anything I could imagine. Hope in what our future held flourished as the faithfulness of God continued to be displayed around us. Even though answers were few, my certainty that God was going to use our story to encourage others and provide hope grew with each passing day.

That evening after tucking Jesi into bed, I stayed up a few extra minutes to send silent praises to the heavens. Unknown to us were the darker days that were coming, days in which we would need these assurances and promises of God's faithfulness more than ever. My focus this evening was simply to rejoice in the blessings we had received and to hand over the future and what I could never control into His willing and mighty hands.

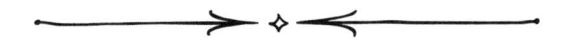

I was now keeping Jesi at home with me in the evenings; so much of my time over the next few weeks was spent in my car, making multiple round trips around the city. I would drop Jesi off at daycare and then travel across town to the hospital to spend a few hours with Josh. I would then drive to the office and work for the afternoon, finishing the day back over at the hospital where I would meet my mother-in-law who had picked up Jesi for me. We ate dinner with Josh, leaving early on those nights when I had to run errands before going home. I did my best to take care of all my responsibilities, but it was physically and mentally exhausting.

Jesi's first day of kindergarten was only a week away, and not a single school supply had been purchased. I could barely contemplate the fact that her father wouldn't be at home to see her off on her big day, let alone gather enough strength to fight the crowds of people at Walmart shopping for their own children. We were all in desperate need of some good news, soon.

And then, it came.

The sky was a magnificent shade of blue that August morning, as though God was painting His promise to us on a brilliant canvas for the whole world to see. The doctors were quick to visit Josh's room, wasting no time in relaying the news to us. I sensed a certainty from them that hadn't previously been there during the testing and waiting periods. One extra doctor was included in the group today. We hadn't seen him for a few days and his presence was an encouraging sight. Dr. Quinn stepped out from the group and walked over to stand beside the bed next to Josh.

"We've completed all of our tests," he said. "We believe you have contracted Guillain-Barré syndrome, which is the reason for the weakness in your lower body." As he continued talking, I fought through the haze to grasp on to the meaning behind the snatches of medical lingo.

"You are very fortunate, Josh. In some cases of this disease, there could be total-body paralysis, but in your instance, it has appeared to stop at your waist. Good news, this paralysis isn't permanent." Josh's doctor walked over and patted his shoulder in encouragement.

"What happens next?" My voice trembled with emotion as the words spilled from my lips.

"Tomorrow, I'll begin a treatment that has proven success with other patients diagnosed with this disease. It is a transfusion of the immunoglobulin from the plasma of blood, commonly referred to in the medical community as 'IVIG.' There is no set number of treatments, but we typically see positive results within three to five rounds."

"And once the treatments are finished, how quickly would you expect to see results?" I asked. "When do you think the nerves will come back? And how soon will he be able to walk again?"

"I can't give you an exact timeframe. The healing process is very slow, and it could possibly take six months to a year or longer for a full recovery from the paralysis. I have faith that Josh will respond well to the IVIG treatments and will eventually make a full recovery." After providing me with a printout that listed some information about GBS, he folded Josh's chart under his arm.

"We'll begin tomorrow," he reassured me with a confident smile and then left the room.

I was aware that the meningitis had run its course. I was aware that Josh was still incredibly ill and that his lower body was most likely paralyzed. What I wasn't prepared for was the reality laid before my feet with the diagnosis. With great effort, I attempted to focus on the positives in this situation, but my heart continued to sink as I listened to the specifics of the disease and recovery timelines.

Guillain-Barré syndrome is an autoimmune disorder in which antibodies in your system begin attacking the myelin sheath that covers and insulates your neurons. The myelin is responsible for protecting the reaction time of your nerve impulses and reflexes. It isn't a contagious disease, but preceded by a viral or bacterial infection, with onset normally occurring one to three weeks after the infection. It begins with tingling or numbness in the feet and then works its way upward through the body as it continues to paralyze.

In some severe cases, it can reach the muscles of the face, eyes, and mouth, leaving the patient completely paralyzed and unable to move, speak, or eat. It can be life threatening if the weakness reaches the diaphragm and restricts the ability to breathe. It can affect anyone, at any age, with no regard to gender, ethnicity, or medical history.

Josh's condition had left him paralyzed from the waist below. The doctors were very confident that at thirty-nine, he was young enough to experience a full recovery, but they were unable to give us a definite timetable for when that might occur. Somehow, his nerves had to remember how to do their job; they would need time to wake up. The recovery process was going to be very, very slow. As thankful as I was to have a diagnosis, I was unsure if the future presented to us would have been better left unknown.

After multiple phone calls and texts alerting the appropriate family members of this recent turn in events, I excused myself from the room for a few minutes, making my way down the hall toward the nearest waiting room. Searching for a place to be alone with my thoughts, I collapsed into a chair closest to the large window overlooking the south side of town. Shock, fear, sadness, and confusion: my emotional roller coaster picked up speed again as my stomach churned.

How could we wait that long?

What would we do?

Would Josh ever be back to normal?

Obviously, I was conflicted. Seeking solace in the only refuge I had available, I picked up my Bible once again, turning to the fourth book of the Old Testament. As I read the story of Moses, I realized that I needed to be patient; answers to the questions I sought would be provided to us in time. My responsibility today was not to dwell in the shadows of fear and uncertainty, but to plead our case before the Lord and wait for His reply. While it might feel like we had been wandering in this unknown wilderness for an eternity, we would not remain there forever. God would take our hand and guide us through to the other side.

*"Moses answered them,
'Wait until I find out what the Lord
commands concerning you.'"*

Numbers 9:8

Moses was responsible for leading several million Israelites out of their bondage of slavery in Egypt, across the Red Sea and into the Sinai Desert, on a journey to the land promised them by God. However, these same people who had just been released from their shackles grumbled and complained incessantly. They were frustrating to deal with, and it was apparent to Moses that they lacked complete trust in what God had planned for them.

They had witnessed the miraculous acts performed in Egypt. The river of blood, the frogs, the insects and flies, the plagues, the hail, the locusts, the three days of darkness, and finally, the death of every firstborn son of Egypt. All this just to move the heart of Pharaoh to permit them to leave. Then, on their departure, the Lord parted the Red Sea, allowing for every man, woman, and child to make it across on dry land. Despite these astonishing events, they still failed to recognize and acknowledge the sovereignty of God.

Only a few days into their journey, the Israelites were afraid Moses had delivered them from the hands of Pharaoh merely to let them die out in the wilderness. They were afraid when their water ran out. Moses pleaded with God and he provided fresh water to drink. They were afraid when their food ran out. Moses pleaded with God and he provided manna for them to eat in the mornings and quail for them to eat in the evenings. Once they reached the foothills of Mount Sinai, they complained that Moses was spending too much time on the mountain with God instead of with them. Moses brought them the Ten Commandments, written by the hand of God himself.

They were afraid when they finally reached the Promised Land because a fierce and giant people already inhabited it, yet God equipped Joshua and Caleb to conquer this new land for them. Even until the very end, they remained uncertain that God would deliver on the promises he'd made. Moses pleaded with them to not be afraid, to stand firm and have faith that the Lord would fight for them. They depended upon Moses for guidance and praised God when their prayers were answered, only to grumble once more when they faced the next hardship.

For each complaint brought before him, Moses turned the situation back over to God before providing the Israelites with an answer. The Lord was faithful to every plea made from this leader of wayward and rebellious people. He knew that the only way they would make it through this wilderness alive was because God was still with them. Despite the many times he had to become the intercessor between God and the Israelites, Moses trusted that God had a plan for their nation.

I reflected back on my own grumbles and complaints I had placed before God over these past few weeks and became instantly humbled and repentant. I was humbled by the faithfulness of God; and repentant of those moments of weakness when my attitude and reactions were more similar to those of the Israelites than I would care to admit.

I declared in that moment to be more like Moses and less like the Israelites. I would raise my hands high in the air when faced with what appeared to be an insurmountable situation and give it all over to God. I would praise Him in my weakness as well as my strength. I would seek His wisdom and learn to wait patiently for the answers.

I would look our future straight in the face and declare that no matter what happened, my trust would be in God.

In the Beginning

Josh's Perspective

Everything that happened to me was so gradual. When the headaches began, we weren't overly concerned. We thought they were related to allergies or possibly stress. It wasn't until the day I was admitted that I knew something had to be seriously wrong. There was so much pain. I couldn't see at all, any type of light hurt my eyes. I felt like I was hallucinating a little bit, and I was afraid of going down the stairs in our house. Maggie called my mom and dad and then the ambulance showed up shortly after they arrived.

Even though I couldn't see, I still heard everything that was going on. I remember being wheeled around on the gurney and hearing the doctors and nurses talking about me and what was happening. I was scared, but the pain was so overwhelming that I could barely focus on anything else. They took me into a room for two separate MRIs, but after that, my memory starts to fade away. I have absolutely no memory of Room 908, or of being in the ICU. Whatever happened during those days is lost to me.

I found out much later, that what little memory I do have of the first few weeks of my illness were actually just hallucinations. One of my first "memories" is an evening that my mom and I were in a bar, singing along to the songs and talking about whether or not we wanted to buy the bar from the owner. Her version of that evening is a bit different. We were singing and laughing, only in a hospital room instead.

My body was awake during the entire episode, but obviously, my mind wasn't quite there yet.

It's hard to describe how I came out of the fog. To me, it felt like I was waking up from a long, extended sleep. At first, you're still really tired, groggy, and disorientated. It takes you a little bit to clear your head. It took a long time for my head to fully clear. It was very intimidating because I still wasn't sure what had happened to me or where I was.

And when I finally did wake up, I had a new reality to deal with. I had so many questions for my wife. Maggie did her best to explain what had happened, but it took me a long time to come to terms with it. Both of us struggled with fear and uncertainty regarding my recovery and how long it would take.

FOUR

DOWN THE PATH OF UNCERTAINTY

*"Saul got up from the ground, but when he
opened his eyes he could see nothing.
So they led him by the hand into Damascus."*

Acts 9:8

It was now the fifteenth day of August. Josh had been in the hospital twenty-five days. I had never dreamed that we would be celebrating his birthday that year while he lay paralyzed in a hospital bed. Josh's one request for his birthday was a steak dinner, and preferably not purchased from the hospital cafeteria downstairs. That evening we dined on takeout placed in styrofoam containers from Longhorn Steakhouse, a meal that was pure delicacy for all of us. As we finished eating, the room began to fill up with friends and family members who came to help us celebrate. At one point there were so many people packed into the small room, the nurses could barely navigate through the crowd.

I glanced around at the friendly faces of those in the room and then over at my husband, whose expression exhibited a weariness only I could interpret. I wondered how he was processing all this. His grip on reality was extremely fragile at the current moment, and while the visitors saw a smiling face conversing with them, they were unaware of how little the "real" Josh was present in those conversations. While Josh may not have been completely himself that night, the most important part was the encouragement and support shown to our family through these visits.

"Happy birthday to you!" Josh's day-shift nurse and her assistant entered his room singing to him while they placed a decorated coffee filter and signed birthday card in his lap.

"I know that you would rather be celebrating your birthday anyplace but in the hospital, so a few of us got together and decided to help brighten your day a little." Josh's nurse walked over to his bed and gave him a hug.

"I've heard rumors that you might be leaving us soon. Tomorrow I'm going on vacation and might not see you when I return." I watched as she wiped a stray tear with the sleeve of her shirt. "We don't want you to stay, because that means you're getting better, but we are going to miss you."

My heart stirred yet again, by the kindness and love that certain staff members continued to show to both Josh and to our family throughout this journey.

After saying good-bye to our friends and family, my in-laws and I visited quietly. Once more, we faced the unknown. The recent diagnosis and subsequent treatments given to Josh by his neurologist had encouraged his doctors that his road to recovery would begin soon. At this point, we faced two separate outcomes based on a choice that was simply not ours to make. This was a medical decision left completely to the mercy of our insurance company.

The first and most encouraging option would be to transfer Josh across the street to the separate portion of the hospital designed for rehabilitation and temporary care. He would be provided with the opportunity for the maximum number of hours available for physical therapy, in hopes of escalating his rate of recovery. In this setting, the possibility of him returning home within a few months was much greater.

The second option was less desirable. If the insurance company deemed him unable to qualify for the rehabilitation unit, they would transfer him to a long-term care hospital, otherwise known as a nursing home. It was discouraging to hear that this option provided the least amount of therapy hours available and could possibly double or triple his recovery time. I was anxious that his full return from the fog would occur within the next few days, and I worried about the effect on his mental health if he were to "wake up" in one of those facilities.

It was more circumstances beyond our control and out of our hands. In this particular situation, I felt utterly helpless. No amount of persuasion or arguing would change the outcome of this decision. There was only One who had any power or control over this moment in our lives. Accepting and acknowledging that fact was my singular recourse.

I received the call while at work the next day. The decision had been made. It was a Friday afternoon, so the paperwork and transfer procedures were rushed into motion in order for him to move before the weekend shift began. I was overjoyed to receive the news that Josh had been accepted into the rehabilitation hospital. It was the option that promised the best outcome for his recovery.

God was faithful yet again.

My steps felt lighter when I left work that evening, as if an enormous burden had just lifted from my shoulders. As I walked across the small parking lot toward the entrance to the Transitional Care Unit, I noticed an unusual quietness about the place. Traveling through the automatic main doors, I was greeted with a hushed stillness. This new facility was only a few blocks away from the main hospital, but the atmosphere of the two buildings could not have been more different. The chaos of the first was now replaced with the quietness of the second.

I turned down the first long hallway I came upon, searching for Josh's new room while my shoes clicked in rhythm on the tiled floor. I heard the distinctive laugh of my mother-in-law, verifying for me their exact location. Entering his room, I noticed the bright smile on Josh's face.

"He just wiggled his toes!" My mother-in-law exclaimed as she rushed over to give me the good news.

"No way!" I replied. Good news of any kind was so rare these days that it took a minute for me to process. I embraced both her and my father-in-law, who had just walked into the room.

"I sure am glad to see you." The smile on Josh's face remained as I leaned over to give him a hug.

After several celebratory minutes of cheering and high-fives, I pulled a chair up next to Josh's bed while the rounds of new nurses and doctors began to make their procession through the room. While he could not provide them with many details about the last few weeks of his life, he was able to clearly answer their questions about his current physical condition.

I noticed that he seemed more aware of his surroundings now. Could it be possible that the fog had finally lifted? Was this change of scenery and renewed sense of hope finally enough to bring him back to us?

We spent the next few minutes reviewing the road map to his recovery with the newest doctor. Josh would need to remain in the transitional unit until his body was physically able to begin therapy. At this point, we still did not have a definitive timeline for his recovery. It could be days, weeks, or even months. All of it hinged solely upon how quickly the nerves in Josh's legs would begin to regenerate. Despite the uncertainty we faced, we continued to rejoice in the small victories. Each wiggle of his toes brought us one step closer back to life.

Josh's parents agreed to continue our arrangement of keeping Jesi with them on Friday nights. It allowed us private time together and now that he seemed more alert, those moments were precious for me. Later that night while I struggled to find a comfortable position on the pullout sleeper chair to review my latest Bible reading, I noticed a silence had saturated our room. Perhaps it was the distance from the constant trauma and urgency across the street. Perhaps it was the decreased amount of interruptions from the nurses in this new section of the hospital. But perhaps, it was just peace.

This peace remained with me as I turned to the book of Acts in my Bible. I was familiar with the story of Saul's conversion to Christianity, but now it came to life for me in a completely new way. Once more, these stories resonated in my life, reassuring and confirming for me that my faith was not in vain.

*"As he neared Damascus on his journey,
suddenly a light from heaven
flashed around him."*

Acts 9:3

Rays of hot sun beat down upon the backs of the group of men traveling down the Damascus Road. Sweat glistened on their foreheads and they were forced to squint in order to focus on the road before them. They had been traveling for several days and were only a short distance away from their intended destination. This morning the leader of the group had risen early, hastily devoured his breakfast of bread and olives, and made his rounds in the camp demanding they be back on the road as soon as possible. The men noticed a renewed energy this morning in the Pharisee they were ordered to protect. The last few days of their journey had been arduous and uneventful; but today they noticed his steps had quickened and his demeanor was more determined as they neared closer to the city of Damascus.

Saul was a man on a mission, the blood of those that followed Jesus fresh in his mind. Only days before he had directed multiple raids throughout the holy city of Jerusalem, rounding up hundreds of these traitorous men and women, imprisoning and torturing each and every one. A sense of urgency compelled him this day to arrive in Damascus as quickly as he could, certain that these followers of "The Way" would continue to spread their disastrous beliefs if he did not reach the city soon.

The group approached the final bend in the road before the long stretch of flat, dusty earth would lead them up to the gates of the city. The midday sun was at its peak high in the sky above them as the group began to weave their way down the road. Saul covered his eyes with his right hand as the sun blazed down upon him. Without warning, a bright light with the force of a thousand suns flashed in every direction around Saul and his men. The effect was so spontaneous that it knocked the men from their horses and forced the entire group to drop face down on the ground shuddering with fear. A loud noise boomed down at them from the sky above, but the words were only distinguishable to one man.

"Saul, Saul, why do you persecute me?"

"Who are you, Lord?" Saul asked.

"I am Jesus, whom you are persecuting," he replied. "Now get up and go into the city, and you will be told what you must do."

As the bright light dimmed, the companions of the Pharisee whose body remained prostrate on the ground before them were stunned and speechless. When their senses finally returned to normal, they rushed around to each member of the group, ensuring that no one had been hurt. Suddenly, the body on the ground began to mumble and make a feeble attempt at standing upright. The men caught each of his elbows, keeping him from falling down yet again. Concerned for their traveling companion, they held tightly to the man whose body continued to tremble.

Darkness. Only moments ago there was sunlight, blue skies, and white clouds. Now there was only black.

Saul was blind.

Alarmed at what had just transpired, Saul's companions led him by the hand for the short distance left until they reached the city. There he would remain for three days in darkness, not eating, not drinking, only weeping and praying. His old life was now gone. Slowly, he would come to discover what his new purpose in life would be after the Lord gave him back his sight and he was filled with the Holy Spirit. He would become the spokesperson for Jesus Christ to the world outside of the Jewish community.

He would become Paul.

Only a few months ago, the life Josh and I had with our young daughter was predictable and ordinary. Then, flashes of light surrounded us and everything changed. The aftermath would bring me a temporarily paralyzed husband, a scared and confused child, and no knowledge of how we would survive the next phase of our lives.

However, like Saul on the road to Damascus, an undeniable encounter with the Holy Spirit would become a defining moment for myself and for our future. There was no going back; the old was now gone. The same God who called out to Saul that day was calling Josh and me to our own new purpose in life; to hold our heads high and our faith higher.

"Mommy, I just want our family back! I want Daddy to come home and I want us to be a family again!"

Sitting next to Jesi in the car, my heart splintered into a million pieces as the words rolled across her lips and tears streamed down her face. With shaking hands and a heart that felt just as broken, I struggled to hold on to whatever sanity I could as we drove home from the hospital. I felt the unsteady ground beneath my feet tremble and shift once more.

I now faced juggling my own emotions along with those of my family, my work responsibilities, becoming Josh's support system, living half my life at the hospital, and essentially becoming a single mom all at the same time. It seemed as if I was auditioning for the circus act that involved spinning multiple plates at one time; would my feeble attempts to keep them spinning eventually end up in an epic crash and burn?

We had done our best to shield Jesi from the painful reality of Josh's present condition, and she had seen very little of him over the past month. Now that we were introducing her to our current situation and the stresses of temporary hospital life, I could feel Jesi's anxiety and fears begin to build with each visit. Her coping mechanisms manifested themselves when she gave attention to everyone but Josh, who would receive only a brief hug from her upon our arrival. The rest of the time, she would sit at a small table the nurses had moved into his room, playing with the Hello Kitty toys and Dora the Explorer coloring books provided for her.

The anticipation of her visits and the subsequent disappointment over her neglect were painfully evident in Josh's demeanor. Each time we arrived and Josh's parents were already there, I could see the agony in his face as he watched Jesi run and jump into my father-in-law's outstretched arms. An aura of rejection clouded every conversation Josh and I had regarding our daughter's behavior.

"I've lost her, Momma. She will barely look at me. I don't think she loves me anymore." The first words he'd whispered to me that evening echoed in my heart.

This breakdown in their relationship was one of the newest challenges we had to face. Before Josh became ill, they were the best of friends, together constantly; going for drives in the country and playdates at the park. Now, because Josh was confined to moving around only in a wheelchair, the interaction between him and Jesi was minimal. Those precious memories of time spent together would become both beacons of hope and painful reminders of what we had temporarily lost.

While my car glided down the road as smoothly as the tears rolling down both our faces, I doubted how I was going to provide reassurances for her demands. How could I encourage her that everything was going to be all right when I couldn't even answer that question myself? We were staring in the face of months of intense physical therapy that would require every ounce of strength and determination Josh had to give. How could I tell her that her daddy would come home soon and everything would go back to normal, when I had no idea of what our new "normal" would look like?

My spiritual focus had become radically refined these past few weeks, yet I found myself again in unknown and uncertain territory. As an adult, I was able to recognize and appreciate God at work in our lives, using our circumstances as an example of His faithfulness. How would I share that wisdom with a hurting five-year-old whose main refuge in life was the solidarity and security found within the loving arms of her mother and father?

I wanted to lie down on the floor and have my own version of a full-blown five-year-old tantrum, but that wasn't an option. I had to locate the source of wisdom on how to deal with this situation as I had every other time. The only way I could stop the spinning was to place my life in the hands of the One who was larger than my fears.

My sorrow and grief were deep as I anguished over the slow erosion of their faith in one another. Neither Jesi nor Josh was able to trust that everything we had lost would return to us one day. They couldn't see that that we had never truly stopped being a family. I needed them to believe that through these trials and hardships, our family would emerge one day like a butterfly from its cocoon; strong and beautiful and complete.

It was the first day of school and excitement buzzed in the air. Squeals and shouts rang out as the children ran back and forth, greeting old friends and comparing new backpacks and lunchboxes. The smallest of the new students stood nervously in line while they held their parent's hand, anxiously peering around the crowd. Jesi stood in front of the sign displaying the name of her school, dutifully posing for her obligatory first-day-of-school picture.

That morning had been a whirlwind of emotions for both of us. She was beyond excited to begin her new school journey. There wasn't a nervous bone in her body as she envisioned new classrooms and new teachers and new playmates. This was the pinnacle of her short life. It was a reprieve from the stresses and anxieties of hospital life and the delicate emotions she had been forced to bear the past few weeks.

My heart held more mixed emotions. I was happy and excited for her, but burdened by the ever-present loss of the other person in her life who should be experiencing this day with us. Josh should have been the one double-checking that her lunch was packed and standing beside her while I took pictures. As heavy as my heart felt, I recognized that Josh was exponentially more weighted down with grief about his absence.

With Josh's move to transitional care, I was able to return to working full days. Driving away from the school, a small trace of guilt washed over me when I felt relieved not to be headed toward the hospital. I was afraid I wouldn't be able to bear the burden of his sadness about missing Jesi's first day of school while trying to fight through my own.

Later that morning on my lunch break, as I carried a bagful of food toward Josh's room, my stomach growled from the smell of chicken nuggets and fries. I tried to focus only on my need to eat and not about whether Josh would ask for first-day-of-school details. I feared any descriptions might send his fragile emotional state back downhill. However, as I entered into his room, all thoughts of hunger or kindergarten vanished immediately. Fear, panic, and pain all converged into one emotion as our eyes locked.

"I feel like I'm being electrocuted!" Josh exclaimed, arching his back in pain.

I threw the bag of food down on a nearby chair and ran directly to his bedside. The next several minutes felt more like hours while wave after wave of unexpected pain swept through Josh's legs. Grasping tightly to his hand, I prayed for relief from this unknown agony. It felt like a bad nightmare had just transported me back in time to those first few days when Josh fought against the pain of the meningitis. Unsure if either of us could bear that scale of pain one more time, tears streamed down my face. A few minutes later, the pain began to ease away and we hoped the worst to be over, only for it all to return shortly with the same intensity.

After frantically dialing the nurse with Josh's bedside intercom, I kept my tight grip on his hand as we prayed together. Responding quickly to our call, Josh's nurse entered his room with a concerned look and a promise to bring pain medicine and his doctor as quickly as possible. Josh's transitional care doctor entered his room only a few minutes later. He was able to provide us with a few answers about these pain-filled episodes and how they fit in with his Guillain-Barré.

He believed the source of the pain wasn't coming from his muscles, but actually from inside of his nerves as his body began the long, arduous fight back from temporary paralysis. He compared it to the sensations felt after a foot or hand had gone to sleep and returned back to full function, only multiplied exponentially. He reassured us that this was actually a good sign, even though it might be hard to see through the pain. Josh's nerves had finally begun to wake up.

The next morning, after weeks of paralysis from the waist down, Josh was able to move one of his ankles. The next day, his other ankle moved. Then it was his lower leg, his knees, and eventually his upper legs. In just a matter of days, we began to see amazing improvements in his movements and flexibility.

His time served in slavery to the temporary paralysis was finally being lifted, however, it brought with it service under a new master. This one was known as depression. In the days following this intense neurological pain in Josh's lower body, he began to feel useless to everyone around him. Even though the nerves had come back, his feet were still lame. He couldn't stand up by himself. He couldn't walk. He couldn't do many things healthy people could. He hadn't seen the world outside the hospital walls in over a month; feelings of isolation and exile threatened every conversation.

One evening during this emotion-filled week, I sat down with my Bible after tucking Jesi into bed, searching once more for solace within its pages. As I read this particular passage in the book of Samuel, I noticed the resemblance between my husband and Mephibosheth. Josh felt exiled from reality, from his relationship with Jesi, and from everything that had previously brought joy to his life. Mephibosheth could not walk, and felt useless to his family as well. They both desperately needed a loving reminder that there was a place saved at the table, just for them.

> *"Mephibosheth bowed down and said,*
> *'What is your servant, that you should notice a dead*
> *dog like me?'"*
>
> *2 Samuel 9:8*

Mephibosheth's eyes focused on the tiled floor beneath his knees, not daring to look up or stare directly into the face of the mighty King David seated on the throne in front of him. Doing his best not to display the fear within his heart, he held shaking hands to both sides of his body. Summoned to appear before the king after living so many years away from the hub of palace life, Mephibosheth could only imagine what the fate of this appearance would bring.

His father, Jonathan, had been one of David's closest friends. King Saul, Jonathan's father and Mephibosheth's grandfather, became jealous of David, fearing he might one day try to claim his throne, and had attempted to take his life. He would not be successful. David received the throne after Saul and Jonathan were both killed during the Battle of Mount Gilboa. Why would King David, after all these years, summon the grandson of Saul, but only to flush out his hiding place and force him to atone for the sins of his grandfather?

"Mephibosheth!"

The single word echoed throughout the entire throne room. Mephibosheth's body was shaking with nerves, his knees threatening to buckle from underneath him. Lame in both feet from a very young age, he had to be assisted into the great room by several of King David's servants. Since he was unable to stand up on his own, the servants helped him up on his knees so that he could bow before the king. If his knees were to buckle, he would surely find himself flat on the floor before the king and his entire entourage. At this point, embarrassment was his last worry. Mephibosheth might find himself without legs or even a life to worry about before the sun set.

"Don't be afraid," David said to him, "for I will surely show you kindness for the sake of your father, Jonathan. I will restore to you all the land that belonged to your grandfather, Saul, and you will always eat at my table."

Mephibosheth's mind was in a daze. He had surely heard that wrong. Daring to lift his head up a few inches, he was curious to see if the expression on the king's face matched with the graciousness of his words. He was surprised by the softness around King David's eyes and the slight upward curve of his mouth as the king's eyes met with the diminutive man bowing before him. What was this mercy that had just been granted? Why would the mightiest king that Israel had ever known choose to pardon a member of the very same family that had attempted to end his life?

Mephibosheth had been five years old when his nursemaid had fled with him out of Jerusalem after news of his father and grandfather's death on the battlefield. He had never known of the close friendship his father had developed with David, nor how bitterly David wept with news of Jonathan's death. He was astonished when King David not only spared his life, but offered him an anointed place at the king's own table.

It was incomprehensible.

It was improbable.

It was amazing.

"What is your servant, that you should notice a dead dog like me?"

Lame in his feet, living most of his life in exile away from the Holy City of his birth, Mephibosheth felt useless to society, useless to himself, and useless to his family; no more than a dead dog. He had done nothing but cower in fear of the fate that might one day appear at his doorstep because of the deeds of his grandfather. He had done absolutely nothing to deserve this unexpected and amazing grace, yet here it was. He could do nothing but humbly accept. The course of his life was about to change.

And then, there was grace.

It came in the form of the pain itself, nudging his nerves back to life. It came in the form of visits from our church family, pouring out their love on to us. It came in the form of the night-shift nurse who would pray over and encourage Josh each evening when everyone else had gone home and the loneliness was the most unbearable. It was in the very presence of the Holy Spirit himself, wrapping his arms tightly around Josh, Jesi, and me as we fought through the obstacles of each battleground.

Similar to David's gift of grace and mercy shown to Mephibosheth that day in a throne room in Jerusalem, it was equally as amazing and incomprehensible to both Josh and myself each time we were blessed through the actions of the people around us. We could do nothing but humbly accept, and like Mephibosheth, our lives would never be the same.

The Days of Recovery

Josh's Perspective

I don't remember thinking "Oh my gosh, I can't move my legs!" I just woke up to that reality. It took a long time for me to process what had happened; it was a lot to absorb. It hurt me to hear about what my family had gone through, watching me suffering as I was.

So many caring nurses and therapists played an important part in my recovery. They were my friends for a time, laughing and sharing stories with me about their own lives and families. I remember one nurse who would come into my room and charge her cell phone during her break. She was a single mom, and we enjoyed talking about our children. Then there was my evening nurse who would pray with me during checkups in the middle of the night. She was one of those people who had a gruff exterior, and might have turned others away, but in reality, she was a very caring person. I also remember the occupational therapist who would come in every day and rub my feet. I wasn't really doing much those days, and it was nice when I did have therapy to keep my mind occupied.

When the neurological pain began, it was very scary. Maggie was with me the first day it started, and neither of us had anticipated the pain or knew how to deal with it. I was relieved to hear the doctor explain what was actually happening; that my nerves were firing back to life. I wasn't going to be permanently paralyzed. It was a wonderful feeling. I began to focus on my recovery and getting over to the rehab hallway as soon as I could.

I was so excited to begin my inpatient physical therapy, but scared to death of some of the equipment I had to use. The standing frame was my arch nemesis. It was probably the best thing for me, but it hurt the worst. I was grateful for my therapists' determination to help me get better, but that didn't take away the pain involved during the process.

One of the hardest things for me to accept during this time was the breakdown in my relationship with Jesi. I couldn't pick her up and give her a hug, or walk down the hallway with her or take her places like we used to do all the time. Even more devastating was the fact that she would barely look at me or talk to me when she and Maggie came to visit me in the hospital. I worried that she would view me as weak and worthless because of my temporary paralysis.

There was so much fear, anxiety, and uncertainty surrounding every new thing I did. I had to relearn how to stand up, pivot my body, and balance my own weight again. Most of the time, it was overwhelming, scary, and frustrating. I pushed myself as hard as I could, but my body was not able to respond as quickly as my mind willed. They were hard lessons learned, but I had to be patient, have faith, and pray.

FIVE

WASHING THE MUD FROM OUR EYES

*"'Go,' he told him, 'wash in the Pool of Siloam.'
So the man went and washed, and came home
seeing."*

John 9:7

Unlike the pain from the meningitis, which only weakened Josh's body, the neuropathic pain was actually serving a purpose. Each day we marveled at the increased flexibility in both his legs and his feet. His doctors and therapists were greatly encouraged by this progress and everyone was anticipating the day he could finally begin physical therapy.

The high point of today wouldn't include a therapy session, but for me, it was just as important. I would be able to take Josh for a stroll outside in his wheelchair. The fatigue of being isolated indoors for such a long period was beginning to take its toll, causing him to become extremely anxious about social interaction. Visiting the outdoors was essential for his mental health.

This was a good time to venture out: weekends were very quiet in this section of the hospital. During the week, the hallways buzzed with patients coming and going from outpatient surgeries and recovery rooms. On the weekends, the only traffic was family members visiting loved ones in either the transitional or rehabilitation units. In between the units were several walled brick courtyards for patients and their families to enjoy.

Reaching the nearest courtyard, I breathed a sigh of relief to see that we were alone in our adventure. Josh wasn't ready to deal with small talk from other patients just yet. His mind had only recently returned to him, and the trauma of his current situation was still too painful to discuss with outsiders. The conversation today would reveal just how much of the past month had truly become lost to him. Down the road, I would understand how that loss of memory was in itself a blessing for him.

I wheeled Josh over to a nice shady spot I had located with a concrete bench I could sit on next to his chair. We spent the first few minutes in relative silence as we both relished in the peace of the outdoors. Birds chirped softly in the tree above us. A gentle late summer breeze caressed our skin. I closed my eyes briefly and for a moment, I could imagine that we weren't in the patio of a hospital courtyard, but sitting in lawn chairs next to Table Rock Lake camping with our family. Breaking the silence, Josh startled me when he spoke.

"What happened to me? Why did this happen? Why?" He repeated this series of questions several times, as if he was also asking them of himself.

"Well, to put it simply, you had a very severe case of viral meningitis that gave you the Guillain-Barré, which paralyzed you from the waist down," I replied, acting as if we hadn't already had this conversation several times.

"Do you remember any of what happened to you over in the main hospital?" I continued, pressing him to see how much he could actually recall.

"I remember riding in the ambulance to the hospital and sitting in the emergency room when they did the spinal tap on me. Then, the next thing I remember is waking up in the room where I am now, not able to walk." He shrugged his shoulders in confusion.

During this conversation, my eyes were open to how little he actually remembered. The pressure on his brain and the pain from the meningitis had eradicated all memories after the first day of his hospitalization. The subsequent volumes of pain medication administered during the first few days twisted any memories he did have into hallucinations. He was talking to people who weren't there and seeing animals scurry around in the corners of the room. He didn't remember being in the ICU, his birthday celebration, or the friends and family who came to visit. He confessed to not saying anything about this to me earlier because it was embarrassing to admit.

"I almost died, didn't I?" The words hung in the air between us as he glanced over at me for confirmation. I nodded my head in response, unable to verbalize the answer.

All those times during the early days where I had believed he was feeling better, and I was hopeful for a quick recovery, hadn't been genuine. I silently grieved for the prospect of what could have happened and rejoiced that it didn't.

"But why did this happen to me, what did I do to deserve this?" The cycle repeated itself once more as Josh continued to push me for answers.

Josh searched for reasons; I searched for wisdom. So much in our lives seemed without explanation or resolution. Why had his relationship with Jesi deteriorated so drastically? When would he walk again? Would our lives ever be the same again? During the next several weeks, in weaker moments of self-pity, both of us would wallow through the mud of these questions.

I was just as uncertain as Josh was about what the future held for him and for our family. The only tangible offerings I could provide him with were those promises delivered to both of us by God.

He would protect us.

He would provide for us.

He would bring us through and heal our family along the way.

After our brief adventure into the outdoor world, fatigue set in and Josh requested that I take him back inside to his bed. Unfortunately, the only safe way to move him between his bed and his chair was with the use of a motorized device known as a sling lift. The room he was currently housed in didn't have an electronic lift installed in the ceiling, so the nurses had to utilize a freestanding lift when he needed to be moved.

Bubbles of anxiety built in my stomach as the female nurses wheeled the lift into his room that evening. From my viewpoint, the lift did not appear to be very strong, and I was completely unsure that this piece of equipment could safely bear the weight of Josh's body. Trusting that the nurses knew what they were doing, I held my anxious thoughts in check before speaking too rashly. I watched as they locked the belt around his waist, pulled him up out of his wheelchair, and slowly attempted to place him in the lift. The next few moments would prove my previous fears true.

My eyes widened as I watched the nurse barely miss the lift seat with Josh's body as she held tightly on to his belt. Stumbling forward, the nurse, along with Josh and the lift itself, crashed to the side. Thankfully, his bed was located in the direction of their fall, catching all three of them. Before I could utter a single word, his nurse bounced directly back up, untangling him from the lift and ensuring he hadn't been harmed. With humiliation and shock written all over her face, she profusely apologized to both of us. She immediately called a few other nurses into his room to begin packing up his personal belongings and move him across the hallway to another room with a preinstalled electronic lift.

That evening at shift change, the nurse who had been in charge of moving him came into his room with tears in her eyes, apologizing again for the earlier mishap. We reassured her it was only an accident and tried to encourage her that one day we would look back on this memory with laughter. Seeing her genuine regret and concern, we exchanged more encouraging smiles and hugs before she left. Later that night, I took a few quiet moments to praise the Lord that Josh wasn't harmed during this episode. If he had sustained injuries, it could have caused a major setback in his recovery.

The darkest moments for Josh came late at night. With the hospital quiet and visitors gone, he was alone with only a blanket of mine and a few of Jesi's drawings taped to the wall, to remind him of home. Hospital regulations required vital checkups on his heartrate and blood pressure every few hours, rendering a full night of sleep nearly impossible. Overcome by homesickness, Josh found very little to comfort him during these wearisome hours, except for one special nurse.

Empathizing with his situation, she would hold his hand while they prayed together, encouraging and comforting him. She was a blessing in disguise, placed in Josh's life to help him when I could not.

Fridays were extra special because I was able to spend the night at the hospital with Josh. This Friday, I was able to witness the compassion of his overnight nurse firsthand. I awoke to soft light and murmured prayers as she helped adjust his blankets and pillows and took his vitals. She was gone within just a few minutes, and I could hear his soft breathing as evidence that he'd returned back to sleep. I thought of all the angels God had placed in our path along this journey, each one of them a reminder of His faithfulness.

A smile crossed my lips just before my eyes closed into my own peaceful slumber. I envisioned a roomful of angels standing watch over Josh and me, their arms spread wide and faces lifted up to the sky in silent praise of the One who stood watch over us all.

———— ❖ ————

I woke up early the next morning with eagerness for the day to come. September was in full swing, and brought with it the much-anticipated college football season. Josh was a dedicated fan of the Arkansas Razorbacks and a few of his cousins were Alabama Crimson Tide fans, producing a friendly rivalry with each new season. This new room held one superb advantage besides being large enough to accommodate several people at once. Four television sets were set into the ceiling because the room had originally been designed to house four patients at a time. These rooms were now private, but still allowed patients to watch each television or all four at one time, if they wished.

Today was family football Saturday in Josh's room. The hospital staff had granted us permission to invite his family, which included cousins, spouses, children, and in-laws. This would be the first time the entire family was back together since Josh had become ill. His birthday a few weeks prior had been the last large gathering, but he had been much too fatigued to enjoy it. I rejoiced this morning, knowing how emotionally uplifting it was for him to have visitors, especially in a setting filled with the familiar jabs and jokes of friendly football competitions.

A few hours later, family members began streaming into his room. Laughter abounded as the young children ran around the spacious room playing together. Relatives cried tears of joy when they saw with their own eyes the progress Josh was making, and how much clearer his mind was now that the fog had lifted. Sunlight streamed in from the large windows on the west side of the room. Each family member shouted and clapped as the various games blared on the screens overhead. Sitting next to Josh that day, I stored away every smile and laugh.

The heartache began as the last person walked out the door and I prepared to return home. One night together never seemed to be enough for either of us, but my Saturday nights now belonged to Jesi as I struggled to balance quality time between both her and Josh. The questions flooded out as I headed for the door.

"Why did this happen to me?"

"What have I done to deserve this?"

"Why can't I go home like everyone else?" Fear and uncertainty pooled together in Josh's eyes.

"You will be able to go home, just not yet. It wasn't your fault and there's nothing that you have done to deserve this, it was just a virus that attacked your body and opened the door for the GBS." I turned to Josh, trying to remain calm and collected. "You have survived so much already. You will make it through this, and Jesi and I will be right beside you every step of the way."

"I know. I pray every night for strength, but when you aren't here with me I get really lonely. It's so hard to stay strong sometimes," Josh replied, lowering his head down to meet his chin.

It was a theme destined to repeat itself. Our days would begin with smiles and end with tears. We would cycle through his repetitive inquiries and my subsequent responses, as both of us battled against the longevity of this disease. For both of us, there were days when we were encouraged by the blessings revealed to us through the healing of Josh's nerves. We celebrated by sharing with friends and family members how we continued to praise God for each answered prayer. Then, we would encounter those moments of fear and doubt when we questioned relentlessly the reasons behind the struggles and shook our heads at the possibility of making it through to the other side.

I kept the onslaught of emotions at bay that evening until after Jesi had gone to sleep. Sitting in Josh's chair in our upstairs family room, I finally let them release as I picked up my Bible to the book of John and read over the story I had chosen for today. The reasoning behind my repetitive answers to Josh's inquiries served a double purpose. I wanted to not only encourage him, but also to constantly remind myself that there was still hope for our future.

Josh would walk one day; the doctors had assured us. On that day, both of us would jump up and down in celebration, just like the blind man healed by Jesus.

*"His neighbors and those who had formerly seen him begging asked,
'Isn't this the same man who used to sit and beg?'"*

John 9:8

Flashes of vivid color.

It was the first thing the blind man noticed as he finished washing the mud from his eyes. Everything was so brilliantly bright; he covered his face with his hands while his eyes finished adjusting to the light. Still cautious of what had just happened, he slowly widened his fingers, peeking through the small openings at the beautiful canvas that sprang forth on the other side of his hands.

Blind from birth, the man was unable to see the crowds shuffling toward him, but his heightened sense of hearing had alerted him to their arrival. He heard the scuffle of feet and buzz of conversation as the group emerged before his begging place just outside the gates of Jerusalem.

"Rabbi, who sinned, this man or his parents, that he was born blind?" Jesus's disciples asked.

"Neither this man nor his parents sinned," said Jesus, "but this happened so that the works of God might be displayed in him."

After hearing this conversation take place between the men who had stopped directly in front of him, the blind man startled as Jesus leaned down and applied a small portion of mud on each of his eyelids. He was then given directions to go to the Pool of Siloam and wash the mud from his eyes.

Without pause or question, the blind man immediately jumped up and ran straight for the water. It was then, as he began to clear the packed earth from his eyes, he realized he was now able to see. His celebrations began in earnest. Jumping, leaping, and running back and forth as the colors began to focus, his shouts of joy could be heard by everyone within earshot. His friends, his neighbors, those whom he used to sit with and beg for coins at the gates of the city were all amazed at this seemingly miraculous event. There could be no other explanation for it.

It had to have been a miracle.

Of course, there were doubters. Some claimed he was the same blind man they had known previously, while others scoffed and frowned that such miracles could take place, discarding them as foolish. They claimed the man only looked like the blind man they had known for years. Surely, it could not have been him! The Pharisees felt they needed further explanation and brought the man into the temple for questioning, demanding answers.

"What have you to say about him?" they asked.

The former blind man could only answer their questions with direct honesty.

"Whether he is a sinner or not, I don't know. One thing I do know. I was blind but now I see!"

Even though Jesus had performed miracles in their very presence, some of the Pharisees didn't believe he was from God. They doubted. They questioned. They shook their heads at the young man from Galilee who dared to disrupt the status quo of the Jewish community. There were rules to follow and reasons for those rules. They were not able to recognize the bigger picture of the grace of God, playing out before their very eyes. My only hope was that in the end, we would endure with the hope of the blind man rather than with the doubts of the Pharisees.

SIX

THE PROMISE OF A PRAYER

"Now, our God, hear the prayers and petitions of your servant. Do not delay, because your city and your people bear your Name."

Daniel 9:17, 19

Two days after our football party, I was at work when the picture popped up on my phone. Taken from Josh's cell by one of his nurses, it showed my husband standing up straight with the help of a device known as a standing frame. I was in awe. It was the first time in two months he had even attempted anything like this. Physical therapists use these frames, which are typically made of black metal with cushions located around the knee and chest areas, to assist patients with spinal cord or other neurological disabilities. For those with permanent paralysis, this might be the only opportunity they have to stand up. In Josh's case, his body would never begin to heal if he didn't reintroduce his muscles to their former functions.

The physical therapists working in the transitional care unit were limited by the scope of their responsibility. The work they did was meant to be preparatory and not strenuous. Their job was to reintroduce their patients' bodies back to normal movements. Some of the exercises included stretching and massaging Josh's legs and tossing a beach ball back and forth. To Josh, these exercises seemed trivial, but he understood that he had to gain his strength back first. Once his doctors felt his body was prepared for the next stage of therapy, he could begin using the exercise bicycles, arm machines, and parallel bars in the rehab gym two hallways down from his room.

It was hard for me to focus on my work after seeing the picture of Josh in the standing frame, and I joyfully shared it with several of my coworkers. We had both dreamed of this day as we neared the two-month point of his hospitalization. We clung desperately to hope and rejoiced in every victory, big or small, taking nothing for granted. The simple act of his standing upright for ten minutes represented the beginning of possibilities for us. As Josh's stay in the hospital increased, so too did his desire to get better and return to a normal life. He wanted nothing more than to go home, and he began using this desire as a catalyst for motivation. He had determined that he would do whatever it took to reach that goal.

Later that day, we celebrated his experience with the standing frame over fresh-baked cookies from Subway. I joined him in a light-hearted moment when one of Josh's motivational tools passed by his doorway. Another patient, much older than Josh and wearing a very loud floral print shirt, would walk up and down the hallway several times a day pushing his own wheelchair. I could see the determination glistening in Josh's eyes as he jealously watched the older man pass by. I knew how much he wanted that for himself, and I was proud of him for attempting to overcome his depression and sadness with bits of humor.

Even though he did his best to keep his head held high and focus on the progress and blessings, the setting of the sun each evening would bring with it the fears and loneliness he fought so desperately to avoid. Before I left to go home, Josh confessed to me about his most recent fears.

"Everything is happening so slowly. I'm afraid that I'll be here forever before I get the opportunity to move over to rehab. I'm scared. Scared that I won't be able to go home soon and scared that I'll be like this for the rest of my life."

"You're not going to be like this forever," I said, trying to remain confident. "The doctors have assured us that you'll make a full recovery, eventually. It's just going to take time."

"I love you very much, I'll see you tomorrow." We exchanged hugs and I left his room, tears pooling in my eyes as I walked down the hallway toward the exit.

Several weeks into his stay at the transitional unit, he feared that while his mind and willpower continued to gain strength, his body was not yet to the point where it could handle the strenuous work required of him in the rehab unit. For Josh, physical therapy and rehabilitation equated to his return home. Going home was what he hoped for more than anything else.

Late that evening I used my quiet time to reflect on the day's events. I pulled up the picture on my phone several times, in awe of the progress Josh was making even though it was excruciatingly slow. I remembered my initial excitement of seeing him standing up and marveled that one small act could represent so much hope for his recovery. I opened my Bible to the book of Mark and read another story filled with excitement. I can only imagine what the disciples Peter, James, and John felt when they witnessed Jesus transform into a vision of his true holy being. I pictured how easily their enthusiasm dampened when Jesus reminded them not to share what they had seen with anyone else. The disciples might not have understood Jesus's instructions at the time, but that didn't deter them from their faith.

*"Suddenly, when they looked around,
they no longer saw anyone with them except Jesus."*

Mark 9:8

The sky was a stunning shade of blue as Peter, James, and John followed the rocky path up the side of the mountain. In front of them, Jesus was leading the way in contemplative silence, a sign for the three disciples known for their boisterous, passionate conversations to follow suit. They were curious about why Jesus had chosen them, while the remaining nine disciples stayed with their tents. Normally, their teacher was leading them straight into the path of the crowds, not directly away from them.

They reached the summit of the mountain in a few short hours. Greeted by nothing but the wisps of winds that circled around them and the chirping of birds in the trees below, Peter, James, and John were thoroughly confused. While they huddled in a circle passionately discussing why they were here, the three failed to notice the abrupt disappearance of Jesus.

A sudden blinding light disrupted their discourse. Shielding their eyes from the brilliance, they began to make out three forms emerging from the dazzling white. Jesus stood before them, clothed in shimmering robes. On either side of Jesus stood Moses and the prophet Elijah. The three appeared deep in conversation when they looked up to see the disciples on their knees in the grass before them, confusion and amazement covering their faces.

After a few silent moments, Peter was the boldest of the three to speak up. Trembling with fear, he haphazardly suggested they erect three shelters on the mountain, in reverence to Jesus, Elijah, and Moses. Out of nowhere, a giant white cloud appeared directly above them and a thundering, explosive voice came out from the cloud, demanding their immediate attention.

"This is my Son, whom I love. Listen to him!"

All three disciples fell instantly to the ground. Trembling in trepidation, they watched the cloud begin to lift from over their heads. Peter cautiously opened his eyes to see Jesus standing in the grass in front of them, a curious look on his face. He reached out his hand to help them up from the ground. Jesus knew this current silence would last for only a few seconds; a barrage of questions from Peter, James, and John was sure to follow.

While the four of them traveled back down the mountain, Jesus hesitated for a moment at a particularly scenic bend in the path that looked out over the green valley below. In a quiet voice, he instructed them to keep the events they had just witnessed to themselves until the Son of Man had risen from the dead.

Following a few paces behind Jesus, the disciples deliberated over the meaning of the curious phrase their teacher had just used. What did "risen from the dead" mean, exactly? Jesus wasn't going to die, so was he referring to Elijah or Moses, whom they had seen only a short while before standing next to Jesus on the mountaintop? They were perplexed at the instructions to wait until this particular event had occurred to share it with anyone else. They wanted nothing more than to run down to the campsite and relay to the rest of their group the amazing details of what had transpired that morning.

Only a short while later they would receive the answers to their questions. Each of them would spend the rest of their lives bearing witness to the death, burial, and resurrection of Jesus Christ. Through them, the gospel would be spread to the ends of the earth and throughout the reaches of time.

I thought back over the events of the past few months; the trials, tribulations, and challenges and how desperately unfair it had seemed at times. Both Josh and I struggled to make sense of it. Then I remembered my encounter with Jesus on the floor of Josh's bathroom. I had seen so much evidence of God's faithfulness demonstrated in our lives.

Everything that Jesus taught the disciples during his ministry on earth was to prepare their hearts and minds for what was to come after his death and resurrection. My confidence began to grow in the knowledge that God had been preparing me for every step of my own journey. He had shown me where I needed to go and what I needed to do. Now, it was my time to begin sharing what I had witnessed with the people in my world.

It was time for me to become His disciple.

A few days later, we had cause to celebrate once again. After three weeks in the transitional care unit, Josh's therapists and doctors were now confident that he was ready to be moved two hallways over to the rehabilitation unit. There, he'd be exposed to three types of therapy, meted out over four forty-five-minute sessions a day. Physical therapy would work with him in the gym to help improve his body movements. Occupational therapy would help with his fine motor skills and hand-eye coordination. Recreational therapy would fine-tune his mental and social skills using various games and activities. Josh would undergo the maximum amount of therapy the hospital allowed.

"I'm worried, Maggie," Josh confessed to me as I began packing up his clothing and toiletries once more for this last move.

"What are you worried about? This is what you wanted, isn't it?" I asked while placing the red blanket I brought from home into a plastic bag.

"Of course it's what I want, but I'm so nervous that I won't be able to perform the work. I'm not sure I could handle being sent back over here to transitional care." He sat in his wheelchair, wringing his hands together in his lap.

Everything Josh would experience from this point on would be new to him; he'd be like an infant learning to use his lower body for the very first time. The paralysis caused by the Guillain-Barré had reset his nerves back to zero. With the help of his therapists, he now had to retrain his body to perform the most basic functions, again. Failure to complete his therapy meant a move back over to transitional care and further away from going home. Failure was not an option for him.

Thankfully, his mood lightened at the appearance of his favorite nurse in his doorway. Being one of the only male nurses in this unit of the hospital, Robert was close to Josh's age and had a similar sense of humor. The two bonded quickly. Robert gave Josh his first official shave just a few days earlier when Jesi made it clear that his facial hair had to go. He was also one of the nurses who would stop by at the end of his shift each evening and check on Josh, even if he hadn't been attending to him that day.

"This is a big move. I'm excited for you, Josh," Robert said as he approached Josh's bed and began transitioning him over to his wheelchair.

"To be honest, I'm kind of nervous, but I know this is what I need to do if I want to go home," Josh replied.

"It won't be long and you'll be walking out of here, telling us all good-bye." Robert's confidence in Josh's abilities was an emotional booster for both of us and helped ease the burden of anxiety we both felt.

I walked slowly in step with Josh's wheelchair as we passed by the transitional care desk, receiving congratulations and high-fives from a few nurses who were excited for Josh's recent move to rehab. Pausing in the rehab gym, which was located between the transitional care and rehab hallways, the three of us took in the surroundings. No therapy sessions were currently scheduled and the spacious room was quiet, the only sound coming from the white noise of the air conditioning in the ceiling above. Josh pointed out the exercise bicycle and arm machines he'd been scoping out during the day. A smile crept up both corners of his mouth as he described each one to me.

Leaving the gym, we made our way down to the next hallway and into his new, private room. The following day the real work would begin, but for now, he would be able to rest and enjoy some quiet time with me.

"I'll stop by tomorrow and check on you," Robert promised as he leaned down and gave Josh a hug.

"See you tomorrow, then," Josh replied with a smile.

Each of these transitions brought with them high levels of emotions for everyone involved. We had been blessed with nurses and hospital staff members whose hearts had been softened by our circumstances and had gone beyond their normal duties to help attend to both of us. It was difficult to say our good-byes to each one, but we knew that with every move, Josh was that much closer to going home.

True to their word, his physical therapists began their work bright and early the next morning. His very first therapy session was to include time in the standing frame. The therapists wanted to evaluate his current tolerance levels, to see where he would need the most work. As we made our way over to the rehab gym, I could see Josh struggling between the joy of finally participating in the work and the panic of realizing he would have to stand in this frame for longer periods than he had in transitional care.

"You're going to do great." I squeezed his shoulder in encouragement as we walked.

"I sure hope so." Josh looked up at me anxiously.

Bedridden and wheelchair bound for over two months, Josh's lower body had lost almost all its muscle memory. The first task he needed to master was the ability to stand up using his own strength. Nervous for him, my hands shook as two therapists helped Josh rise up from his wheelchair. They quickly secured his waist and knees with belts that would support the weight of his body. When Josh placed his arms in front of his body on the upper platform of the standing frame, I watched his smile turn into a grimace of defeat.

"I can't do this." Unable to stand for more than a few seconds at a time, he quickly realized his tolerance level had hit its peak.

After two more unsuccessful attempts, the therapist chose to end his session, not desiring to press his body any further and inflict undue stress upon him. Disappointment and frustration clouded Josh's face as we returned to his room. Exhausted from the therapy, he requested the nurses move him back into his bed.

"I don't want to be sent back." Josh closed his eyes and turned his head away from me.

"This is just your first day. They aren't going to send you back yet." I sat down on the side of his bed, squeezing his hand in reassurance. "Don't give up this easily."

Josh didn't reply. I understood his anxiety. I too, feared a move back to the transitional care unit would cause major setbacks in his recovery time. Both of us needed a distraction. I suggested that we take a few minutes to go outside and sit in the courtyard located just outside of his room.

I located a nice spot in the shade, locking the wheels on Josh's chair before sitting down next to him. For the first few minutes, we sat next to each other in mutual silence, each lost in our own thoughts. Glancing over at Josh's still form, I noticed he had chosen to close his eyes for a brief minute. I took advantage of those seconds to mimic his actions, closing my own eyes and silently crying out in prayer. As I pled our case before the Most High with hands wrung together, I poured out my soul.

I prayed for strength for Josh's body, as it would be tested beyond compare in the days to come. I prayed for solace for his heart and mind that he would be able to find some measure of peace within his current circumstances. I prayed for wisdom for myself. I would need every bit of it as I continued to stand next to and support a husband who was fighting the battle of his life.

That evening during my quiet time, I reflected on my earlier petitions to God out in the courtyard of the hospital. I pulled out my Bible and turned to my chosen verse for the day, a story of the mighty prayer warrior Daniel. Daniel understood that he might not live to see his Holy City restored, but he had no doubt that what God had revealed to him would one day be fulfilled. He placed his trust in God, believing that His word was truth.

Tonight, I needed that reminder that God would be just as faithful in our lives as he was with Daniel.

> *"We and our kings, our princes, and our ancestors*
> *are covered with shame, Lord,*
> *because we have sinned against you."*
>
> *Daniel 9:8*

Daniel lay prostrate on the floor of his living quarters, the midday sun beating down upon his back. His knees ached from the weariness of being in the same position for hours, and he continually shifted his weight back and forth to keep his legs from going numb. He would cry out in prayer, then become overwhelmed with the heartache of his requests and eventually break down into tears. He did not weep for himself, but for his people and for his beloved homeland of Jerusalem.

Recently, after studying the word of the Lord given to the prophet Jeremiah, Daniel received understanding of the fate of the Jewish people, and how long they would continue to suffer in slavery and bondage to the Babylonian Empire. Jerusalem would lay in ruin for a total of seventy years; almost an entire generation. Children would be born, raise families, and maybe even die, all within the walls of Babylon. They would never see the magnificent holy city of their parents' birth. Their birthright and legacy would be merely a story told around the dinner table and at bedtime.

Daniel grieved for this realization. He grieved for the reasons that had brought them into captivity, and he grieved for the city that would remain in desolation until the seventy years was completed. Over the past few years, he witnessed his fellow countrymen adapting and becoming accustomed to the ways of this strange, foreign land. He had seen the heartache produced by slavery. He understood that his people would never truly be free until they returned home.

The sun continued its descent in the sky as Daniel prayed and the trays of food left outside of his door remained untouched. Soft beams from the fading sunlight landed on his neck as he pleaded with God to listen to his petitions. He begged for forgiveness; both for himself and all of Israel. Lifting his head up from the floor, Daniel repeated this request one more time as the tears flowed down his face.

Then it happened. The room suddenly lit up with spectacular light, and Daniel found himself once more on his knees. Leaning down, Gabriel extended an outstretched hand to pull Daniel back up to his feet. With a smile that could light a thousand fires, the messenger of the Lord proudly announced the reason for his visit.

"Daniel, I have now come to give you insight and understanding. As soon as you began to pray, a word went out, which I have come to tell you, for you are highly esteemed. Therefore, consider the word and understand the vision."

He would continue on to explain certain events that were to happen in the future regarding the fate of Jerusalem. The Holy City would be restored one day, but only before each of these events had occurred. After the prophecy had been revealed, the luminous light slowly faded away. The room felt empty once more as Daniel walked over to rest his body against the wall underneath his window. By now, the sky outside was blanketed with stars. He pondered in silence the information that Gabriel had relayed to him. It was overwhelming and hard to comprehend, but he trusted that it was the Word of God, and the truth.

Later that evening as he finished the remaining edible portions of his leftover food, Daniel lifted up praise to the heavens once more. There would be a price to pay, but God hadn't turned his back on his children. They wouldn't be abandoned and left to ruin within the walls of Babylon. Jerusalem would one day be restored and rebuilt. With eyes heavy from a day filled with emotions, the prophet laid his weary body down on his mat and fell into a deep, dreamless sleep.

God was still faithful.

My prayers that afternoon were appeals for the Jerusalem that lay in ruins underneath our feet. The path of recovery stretching out before us was littered with unknowns and uncertainties. Josh was barely able to stand up by himself. Discouraged and frustrated, he fought through the same cycle of emotions every day. I had prayed so much in the past few weeks that my requests seemed to become one big, jumbled mess. Josh was healing, and we had so much to be thankful for, but the strength it required to make it through each day was tremendous.

Despite the temporary paralysis, Josh's life had been spared. His body would recover, but the timeline and pace were not ours to determine. Hope had been revealed to us, and at times, that hope was the only tangible thing we had to hold on to. Our knees would become weak and our legs would fall asleep as we continued to plead our case before the Most High, but we did not have to despair. I had no doubt that God would fulfill His promises to us.

He was still faithful.

SEVEN

ABUNDANCE IN A DEN OF LIONS

*"The king was overjoyed and gave orders to lift
Daniel out of the den. And when Daniel was lifted
from the den, no wound was found on him,
because he had trusted in his God."*

Daniel 6:23

The following day we met Kristi, the newest member of Josh's therapist team, and someone who would become pivotal in his recovery process. Her positive attitude and infectious encouragement drew both Josh and myself in from the start. Kristi would soon become his biggest fan, cheering him on through every move he made and every exercise he completed. She would push him in just the right ways to fuel his desire to get better.

Today's session would include time spent in the rehab gym utilizing several different pieces of equipment in order to gauge what movements his body could currently handle. Sitting down on a bench across from Josh, I watched Jesi bounce around the room. It was Saturday, and no school meant she could join us for therapy today.

"Look Mom, no hands!" She had located a beach ball in the corner of the room and was now balancing it on top of her head. All four of us chuckled as she attempted to bounce it like a soccer ball. She continued to keep the mood light, making silly faces at us while we waited for Kristi to prepare the bicycle for Josh. I was overjoyed to witness her having fun and to see glimpses of the real Jesi shining through. I realized how desperately I missed her contagious humor and childhood innocence; we had seen so little of it since Josh got sick.

After strapping Josh's safety belt tightly around his waist, Kristi helped him pivot from his wheelchair onto the stationary bicycle. As Josh positioned himself on the seat of the bicycle, his lower body trembled. Kristi realized that his legs weren't strong enough to hold themselves up yet, so she quickly ran over to another station and grabbed an extra belt. She wrapped the belt around his knees to keep his legs from falling to the sides.

"Okay, now just focus on lifting your legs up and down. Take it slow; start with one rep at a time." Kristi stood in front of Josh with one hand positioned on the bicycle.

The first few moments were extremely tense as he fought for enough control of his shaking legs to begin moving his feet up and down on the pedals. Finally, his body began to respond to his brain's request for movement. I could see small glimmers of pride forming in his eyes as he pushed through each repetition.

"It's like riding a bike, right?" Josh's playful pun on words brought a smile to my face.

"You're doing great. Keep that pace up for a few more minutes then take a break. I know you're excited, but don't overwork yourself," Kristi reminded him.

While Josh continued his exercise on the bicycle and Jesi played on a footstool behind me, I took advantage of the few seconds of distraction to snap a few pictures. I had refrained from taking pictures of him up to this point, but I felt it was time to begin journaling his progress for later reflection. These memories would be critical for the days when it felt like we wouldn't make it through to see the sun set. They were encouraging reminders that helped ground us to the truth of Josh's recovery.

All three of us were disappointed when his session finally ended, although I could see exhaustion written all over Josh's face. Over time, the stationary bicycle exercises would become one of his favorite because they provided him an enormous sense of accomplishment. Eventually, he would reach a point where his legs gained enough strength to pedal on their own, and no strap around his knees would be required.

Although Jesi and I were able to attend this session with him, most of his workouts would occur during the weekday while I was at work and Jesi was in school. Watching up close as he struggled and then overcame these hurdles was a precious blessing that I didn't take for granted. In those moments, I was able to witness the true power a caring physical therapist can have in the life of a patient. I observed compassion, empathy, and encouragement from these therapists as they saw the people behind the disability and genuinely cared about helping them get better.

Josh's therapist, Kristi, was a prime example of this compassion at work. She encouraged her patients while they physically pushed themselves through each exercise, cheering them on when it got tough and celebrating with high-fives and hugs when they completed each repetition. The bright smile she wore on her face every single day was a testament to both the patients and their families that her greatest joy came not from collecting a paycheck, but from helping others.

During the peak hours of the day, an uplifting and positive atmosphere filled the rehab gym. Music would play over in the corner next to the occupational therapist's desk while patients played games. Occasionally, you would see a therapist begin to dance or sing along with the beat of a song, which never failed to brighten the day of even the unruliest patient.

These therapists understood the importance of a positive and uplifting attitude in the recovery of someone who is scared and hurting. It was evident in how they engaged with the patients as well as in their own demeanor. They loved what they did and it showed. For Josh, their support was a pivotal part of his recovery.

That evening after Jesi and I returned home and I allowed her a few extra minutes of time in the bathtub, I pulled out my Bible and reviewed the scripture that was next on my list. Reading through the second book of Corinthians, I thought about the early church and how the Apostle Paul had encouraged them to look beyond their own circumstances and find a way to bless others. God, who would then provide for all their needs, would bless what they gave of their own abundance. With God's help, their love for others would change lives.

*"And God is able to bless you abundantly,
so that in all things at all times,
having all that you need, you will abound in every
good work."*

2 Corinthians 9:8

The heat of the midday sun beat down upon the backs of people making their way down the long corridor of shops located in the center of the ancient Greek city of Corinth. With her baby locked tightly on her hip, the young mother struggled to navigate through the crowds, keeping both her child and small basket of food safe from the slippery fingers of market thieves who lurked around every corner. The food in her basket represented all that her family would have for the day.

Finished with her purchases, she made her way back down the hill toward the modest house she shared with her husband, infant child, and two other families. Joined together by a common cause, they were all newly converted Christians, baptized by the founder of their church only one year ago. She remembered the Apostle Paul's warm smile and fatherly embrace as he pulled her up out of the river during her own baptism. His passion for Jesus and for the church was unmistakable. She looked forward to when he would return and speak to their congregation again.

Distracted by her thoughts, she barely noticed the diminutive form as she turned the corner, and had to catch herself from stumbling over him and spilling the contents of her basket. The young man's body had become so malformed from the ravages of hunger that he appeared years younger than his actual age. His back leaned against the wall, he looked up at her with sunken eyes and a withered smile. He hesitated a few minutes before deciding that she wasn't going to do him harm and reached out a trembling hand toward her.

"Help me, please," he said with a ragged whisper.

Her heart softened for the pitiable figure standing before her. Orphaned at birth, she understood the heartache of abandonment and the embarrassment of begging for food. She had been discovered in a similar fashion as this young man and rescued by a kind shopkeeper and his wife. In their home, she'd found love and acceptance. Reaching into her basket, she retrieved one bright red apple, a chunk off the loaf of bread, and a small piece of cheese and handed them over.

Genuine surprise glowed in his eyes as the young man reached up and cautiously took hold of the meager offering. Leaving him to his newfound feast, she promised to have her husband and an elder from their church come visit him soon.

Walking down the dusty path toward her home, she prayed that the Lord would provide for the unforeseen reduction in their food supply. She had already prepared her heart to accept a fast this evening, knowing that the needs of her small family came before hers. As she approached the cottage, she noticed an unfamiliar basket covered in cloth sitting on her front step. Lifting it up, she noticed the small fish symbol stitched into the underside of the cloth.

It was the unmistakable sign of a fellow Christian. Someone had felt prompted to leave this offering of food on her step this morning, not realizing that it would be just enough to replenish the supply given earlier to the young man up the street. Tears of joy rolled down her cheeks as she recalled the words of Paul's most recent letter to her church read by an elder just the day before. God was truly blessing her in abundance so her family would always have what they needed and that their work for Christ would never go in vain.

The young man might now have a chance at a new life and an opportunity to learn about the love and grace that only comes from Jesus. She thought of her own parents, who had sacrificed a place in their home for an orphaned child, not realizing that one day the seeds they had sown would reap generously through her. She thought of her own son, who was looking up at her curiously while the tears continued to roll down her face.

She knew that her decision had been the right one.

God be praised.

I realized that the blessings I received from being present for Josh's therapy sessions were actually signs of God at work in our lives, once again. Each pat on the back, each smile, and each hug from his therapists were gentle reminders from God to take the blessings of His faithfulness and turn them into praise. Then, when the praise was finished, to give of the abundance. To go beyond merely acknowledging the blessings but to begin blessing others in turn.

What did I have to give, though, when all my energy and resources seemed consumed by my current situation? At times, I felt utterly helpless, yet I knew that wasn't true. He was requesting me to take a leap of faith, to trust that he would always provide and to turn my blessings into seeds of my own.

I had to keep reminding myself that this season of waiting for Josh to recover could be the season that I needed to prepare my heart and mind for what was to come. As Josh fought through each day of therapy, I fought for every day of hope. We would have everything we needed, at all times.

God would supply.

That would be enough.

I tried my best to be excited about the three-day business trip to Chicago, but as I stood patiently in line waiting to board the plane, vicious knots formed in the pit of my stomach and my heart constricted in anxiety. This trip had been planned earlier that summer before Josh had become ill. I was given the option to cancel; none would have faulted me for it, but I made the decision to go on the trip anyway. Trying to convince myself that I would be fine, my mind had almost believed the ruse until I stepped foot into the large waiting area of the Branson airport.

I had only just begun to reconnect with a husband whose physical ailments had separated his mind from us for over a month. This morning, I was going to get on a plane that would take me several hundred miles away from him. Business trips had always been exciting opportunities for me to travel outside of my normal working routines and a chance for Josh and Jesi to have some time alone together. Stress and anxiety had never played a part before. Now, I worried that I had made the wrong decision and three days of separation from my family might be more than I could handle.

My coworkers and I were positioned in the back of a large group of people waiting to board. No surprise that on a busy Monday morning the plane was booked full and the only seats left were those that had to be hunted for. Spotting the first available space, I politely nodded toward two passengers already seated and requested enough room to navigate between them to the middle seat. As I sank down into the seat, I fumbled to retrieve my headphones from my purse and hastily plugged them into my phone.

Inhale. Exhale.

Focusing on my breathing, I fought desperately against the twin terrors of anxiety and claustrophobia. A minor emotional breakdown seemed to be positioning itself on the horizon of my heart, mocking me, reminding me that for the time being, there was absolutely no place to hide on the plane. Like it or not, I was going to have to deal with the threatening tidal wave of emotions one way or the other.

I closed my eyes and invited the encouraging lyrics of "Oceans" by Hillsong United and "Praise You in This Storm" by Casting Crowns to produce waves of hope and peace that would crest higher than the flood of anxiety and fear I was facing. I sought after the reminders that even though my situation seemed to be spiraling out of control, there was One who had been in control the entire time.

Late that evening after we returned to the hotel from dinner, I called my mother-in-law to check in on Jesi. My heart ached as I heard her small voice happily chirping over the phone while she informed me about what she learned at school that day. I told her good night and then dialed Josh's phone next. Taking a deep breath, I prepared my heart for the next conversation, which would not be as joyful as the first.

"I wish you were here with me. I miss you so much already." The heartache was evident in Josh's voice when he answered the phone.

"I'll be home before you know it," I replied confidently, trying to sound positive.

"I'm just so used to you being here with me in the evening. I'm no good without you," Josh said. In that moment of raw honesty, I realized how much my husband depended upon my support, encouragement, and physical presence to make it through each day.

"Let's say a quick prayer together. Maybe that will help both of us feel better?" I suggested. The prayer granted both of us a sense of peace, and we chatted a few more minutes about the weather and my travel experiences. I finally hung up the phone, but realized that I wouldn't be able to sleep for a while. I pulled out the Bible packed away in the side compartment of my luggage. Opening up to the book of Daniel, I forced my thoughts away from the earlier heartache and into the amazing story of a man who spent the night with lions.

My temporary self-inflicted prison on the airplane earlier that day paled in comparison to what Daniel had to endure spending his evening with the lions. I had made the choice to travel that day; Daniel's confinement was not of his choosing. I was able to escape the temporary confinement once the plane landed. Daniel had to remain patiently in prayer until the morning dawned and the king hastily made his way down to the chamber to see if he had survived.

> *"So the king gave the order, and they brought Daniel and threw him into the lions' den. The king said to Daniel, 'May your God, whom you serve continually, rescue you!'"*
>
> *Daniel 6:16*

Daniel heard the scraping sounds of the large stone as it was rolled back over the entrance to the dark chamber. The only light provided was from a small round window set into the wall far above his head. The air was damp and stale, as if even the breeze had found itself a prisoner of the king. Standing with his back against the cool stone, Daniel's eyes fought to adjust to the surrounding darkness. He couldn't see the great beasts lurking in the corner of the chamber, but their presence was fully known merely by their ragged breaths. A low snarl began from the corner and worked its way around the room, as if the lions were conversing with each other about this new visitor.

The last words spoken by the king still echoed in the air. The anguish in the king's eyes was palpable as he stood before Daniel.

The king was accurate in his assessment of Daniel's faith. He did serve God continually. Multiple times during the day he could be found in his private room, on his knees pouring out his heart and soul in thanksgiving to God. It was no secret to anyone whom he swore allegiance to; he had never pretended otherwise. Although his loyalties lay first with God, he also served his king with honesty and integrity. While it didn't surprise Daniel to find himself suddenly imprisoned in what seemed an impossible situation, the king whom he had served loyally and faithfully was not quite so certain of the outcome.

Sinking down into a seated position on the stone floor, Daniel's heart was heavy for the sleepless night he was sure his king was about to endure. He placed his head in his hands and began to pray. Another rumble emerged from the darkness as the beasts made their presence known. With eyes still closed and words of praise rolling off his tongue, Daniel sensed movement in the darkened chamber.

Warm, stale breath invaded the space around his body. Not daring to move a muscle, he felt a small tickle of whiskers against the edge of his arm. He heard sniffing noises coming from the beast as it continued to survey his body. The prayers he had begun minutes before continued in silent earnest as the lion paced back and forth in front of him.

Daniel trusted completely in God's plan, but he couldn't predict how the night was going to end. There were only two possible outcomes in this situation. Even though he knew he was innocent and didn't desire to die as a meal for these great beasts, he still prepared himself for that possibility. After a few more minutes of sniffing, the lion turned around and sauntered back over to join the other beasts. It released one more guttural growl, circled the small space on the floor, and lay back down.

Cautiously opening one eye and peering out from between his arms, Daniel was stunned to see that a soft white light emanating from the corner where the lions slept now surrounded him. A lone figure stood in between the beasts with both of his hands resting on top of their heads. The angel leaned down to touch each of the lions' muzzles, as if he was merely petting a domesticated feline. The snarls that had been present since Daniel's entrance into the chamber became silent while the lions settled into a peaceful slumber.

The light slowly faded away, and with it the angel sent to close the mouths of the lions. No harm would come to Daniel this evening. God had preserved his life. Feeling secure enough to stand up and stretch out his limbs, he spent the next few hours praising God. While he worshipped, Daniel could hear the light snores of the lions in their corner of the chamber. He was overwhelmed once more and in awe of what had transpired that evening.

What I was not able to escape and what no amount of mileage could erase was the unknown future staring Josh and me in the face. The fear of it had become our own personal lion, sniffing in curiosity around the outermost regions of our faith, testing us for even the faintest sign of weakness. It paced back and forth, snarling each time our defenses were down, whispering lies and deceit into our ears. It tried to convince us that we really weren't strong enough to make it through this trial.

Then, with only a breath of a prayer, the angel of light would make his appearance, point his finger at the lion, and shut its mouth once and for all. The beast would be silenced and reminded who was really in control. Darkness would never win this war, and fear would never be our king.

EIGHT

THE GROUND BEGINS TO SHAKE

> *"Suddenly there was such a violent earthquake that the foundations of the prison were shaken. At once all the prison doors flew open, and everyone's chains came loose."*
>
> *Acts 16:26*

Josh would be coming home. He had received official confirmation of his discharge date while I was in Chicago. The text message from my mother-in-law was the first thing I noticed as I turned my phone on after our plane landed. I was overjoyed to hear the news. This was it—a tangible sign that Josh's recovery was progressing. Procuring a ride from the airport directly to the hospital after I had retrieved my luggage, my heart felt lighter than it had in weeks. The separation from my family the last few days had been excruciating; but it did provide a unique opportunity that would not have happened, had I not gone through with the trip.

I had the chance to see myself away from the stress of hospital and workloads and mounting responsibilities.

Discussing our situation and the progress Josh was making over dinner at Giordano's pizza restaurant, I was able to answer inquiries from co-workers honestly. Some had been following our story from the beginning, others had not been aware of the situation at all. I could hear myself from a third-person perspective, telling about the heartache, the fear, and the unknowns, but then following through each one with a similar story of faith.

I realized that the abundance God was gently guiding me to give was something that I had the most to offer at this point in my life; an abundance of hope. I witnessed the power and inspiration a simple confession of fear and uncertainty combined with a copious amount of faith could provide. As I shared, others found themselves relating to our story in some way. Almost everyone I talked to had a friend or family member who had suffered through a serious medical condition. Although the specifics were always different, the underlying elements remained the same. As human beings, we are all searching, in one way or the other, for something to believe in. Through this experience, my faith had been refined, yet again.

Later that evening, my excitement began to build as I walked through the parking lot toward the hospital entrance. Grasping the cool metal of the door handle, the first thing to greet my senses was the ubiquitous smells and sounds of the hospital. As I rounded the corner, my heart filled with joy to see my family.

"Mommy, you're home!" Jesi exclaimed when she saw me enter the room.

My heart melted when I heard the exhilaration in my daughter's voice. She ran across the room in total abandon, and her exuberant embrace brought with it tears of joy for both of us. Holding tightly to my legs, she begged me not to leave her for that many days again. I glanced over at Josh as I gently kissed the top of Jesi's head, and I could see the same request mirrored in his own eyes. I reached over and wrapped my arms around his neck, praising God for this blessed reunion.

Every Thursday my husband's parents would bring dinner to the hospital, creating "Allen Family Night." For a few hours each week, laughter would replace tears; fellowship took the place of fear and anxiety. It was a taste of normalcy.

Seated around the table that evening with good food and laughter abounding, I could sense that none of us wanted the special time to end. These moments of levity and happiness were too rare for our family. Each of us found ourselves at different places in discovering how to find and keep true joy during even the darkest of times. Learning to appreciate the blessing of a simple family gathering was a good starting place. These dinners would become a celebration of another week of perseverance, and a sign that we were that much closer to the biggest celebration of all.

Before Jesi and I left that evening, I recognized a newfound determination in Josh's eyes whenever he mentioned his discharge date. His goal from the very beginning, after the fog of his mind had begun to clear, was to make it back home. I rejoiced with him, but thoughts began to drift around in the back of my mind about what life would be like for him when that goal was accomplished. Things wouldn't be like they were before he got sick, and I was afraid of how disappointed he might become.

That evening before I fell asleep, I consoled myself within the pages of the Bible as I had done so many nights before. Opening to the book of Acts, I was encouraged by the scripture I had selected to read. The walls that shook that day in Philippi were physical ones, but the events that transpired in the prison altered more than just the brick-and-mortar structure. Because of Paul and Silas's faith, the Lord chose to use a simple act of nature to transform lives.

> *"The jailer called for the lights, rushed in, and*
> *fell trembling before Paul and Silas.*
> *He brought them out and asked,*
> *'Sirs, what must I do to be saved?'"*
>
> Acts 16:29

Madness. Confusion.

Shouts were heard coming from the marketplace while curious Philippian citizens made their way through the growing crowds toward the center of activity. The local magistrates stood next to each other on the raised platform in the middle of the market square, faces distorted with indignation and fists raised in the air, shouting their proclamations above the noisy crowd. The citizens who had just joined the commotion struggled to see the focus of these accusations. They saw two figures standing in the dirt before the platform, their stances firm, their eyes locked squarely on the magistrates as they announced their sentences.

The punishment was swift and severe. Immediately stripped of their cloth tunics, the men were subjected to a brutal public flogging. Bruised and bleeding, they stumbled behind the guards leading them toward the gates of the prison. The other prisoners hurled insults at them as they passed by each cell.

"Watch these two very carefully, or else!"

The jailer's eyes widened in curiosity at the guard's orders as he silently appraised his new inmates. Neither of the men looked to be in any condition to harm anyone. Wondering what heinous crimes they had committed to place them under his care, the jailer opened the door to the innermost cell of the prison. Shaking his head as he turned the key to the stocks in the floor that fastened to their ankles, he glanced up into the eyes of the man he was shackling. The middle-aged man smiled at him with a warmth that startled him to the core.

Late that night after he made his final rounds and to secure the prison, the jailer lay down on his straw mat, closing his eyes in exhaustion. Dreams came quickly this evening. Tossing and turning in his sleep, he dreamed of the strange prisoners shackled in the innermost cell. He could hear them singing, clapping their hands, and bobbing their heads back and forth in praise to an unseen god while the other prisoners sat quietly in their cells listening.

Unusual, indeed. Suddenly, the ground beneath the jailer's mat began to tremble with intense force. Jumping up from his bed, he found himself pitched forward as a violent tremor shook the very foundations of the prison. Dust fell down from the brick walls and ceiling, and he brushed it away from his face. Then, as quickly as it had come, the earthquake was gone. Once the trembling subsided, the jailer was welcomed with a sight even more disturbing than the cracks below his feet.

All the prison doors were open.

Sickened by the sight of the empty cells, he knew what must happen next. There would be no trial for his crime. With his sword drawn, he accepted the penalty for his actions.

"Wait, don't harm yourself! We are all here!" the Apostle Paul shouted in desperation to the jailer about to take his own life.

Silas knelt down next to the trembling man, encouraging him to drop his sword. He pointed to the prisoners who had not escaped but had chosen to remain in the cell with Paul. The jailer listened to the prisoners recount the events of the past few minutes. There was no doubt in his mind that what Paul and Silas spoke was the truth. He needed no other confirmation than to see that not one prisoner had escaped during the confusion of the earthquake.

The walls of Josh's hospital confinement had begun to shake. Our existence altered as the ground beneath our feet trembled. Yet, once the trembling had finished, we remained. We chose not to escape, but to stay in our cell waiting for God to provide us with directions. To make it through, we would need every bit of His guidance, strength, and love.

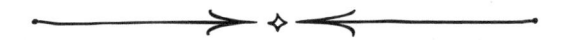

Three days before Josh was discharged, I stood on the sidewalk outside the main entrance to the rehab hospital, with butterflies circling in the pit of my stomach.

"Maggie, you stand here, in front of Josh. Angle his wheelchair toward the open door and make sure to position your legs between his. Then grab the belt around his waist with both hands as Josh lifts his body up and places himself on the board. Use the belt to balance his body and guide him into the car."

I listened with trepidation as Josh's therapist, Kristi, explained how I'd be helping transfer him in and out of our car with the use of a smooth wooden board called a "slide board." Sensing that we were both nervous, she had us repeat the steps several times to ensure that we felt comfortable with the process. I had witnessed Josh's nurses use this board many times when they were transferring him from bed to wheelchair in his room. However, in just a few short days that responsibility would now be on my shoulders. There would be no trained professionals at our house to help me. This realization made the butterflies tumble even more.

Josh could barely stand, and he wasn't able to walk yet. That was the most difficult and disappointing reality check of them all. We had prayed for complete healing and held out hope each day, but unfortunately, Josh's nerves weren't ready yet. Necessary preparations were now required in our home to account for the extra space his wheelchair would require. Family members had spent several hours the past weekend helping me clean and rearrange furniture in our house to make it more wheelchair accessible. My father-in-law had spent days constructing a new wheelchair ramp adjoined to our front porch so that we could bring Josh in and out of the house safely.

Being unable to walk meant that access to our upstairs living space would be restricted. Josh would have to reside solely in the downstairs section of our house until his muscles regained enough strength to be able to walk up the stairs. We rearranged a room adjacent to our living room to accommodate a bed for him to sleep in.

My confidence floundered with each final visit from his team of doctors. They had specific instructions on how I was to care for Josh's medical needs, from dry shampoo for his hair because he wasn't able to stand up in the shower, to the wound care and dressings for his bedsore. Clinically, his doctors had determined his recovery had progressed enough that constant supervision wouldn't be required when he returned home. We had arranged for weekly visits from a local home health-care agency to check on the status of his bedsore. It was a relief to learn that their nurse would be available on call if needed, but it was still overwhelming to think that the primary care responsibility would be mine to bear.

How would I handle the stress of working full time, taking care of household responsibilities, getting Josh to his weekly doctor's appointments on time, helping with his medical and emotional needs, as well as caring for Jesi? The weight of this tremendous burden bore down upon me.

I did everything I could to let the excitement and joy of his homecoming override these insidious fears. Jesi was only five and she needed to see her family back together again. My husband was fixated on the hope of returning home, and I didn't want to burden him with any suggestion of negativity regarding that reunion. I could feel the increased love and support from friends, family members, coworkers, and church members as the day grew closer. Their prayers were uplifting and encouraging, but I still fought against a terrible sense of loneliness. The battle with my stress was intense. Clearly, I'd need some extra armor for this particular conflict.

The night before Josh came home, I tossed and turned for hours, unable to reach a deep sleep. Staring at the dark ceiling, I suddenly realized that I had neglected to read my appointed Bible verse before I went to bed. Crawling quietly out from under the covers, I tried not to disturb Jesi as she slept soundly.

I retrieved my Bible and sat in our upstairs living room, opening to the passage I had selected. It was the story of the faithful Jewish remnant returning to Jerusalem after their seventy-year captivity in Babylon. For the Jews forced into exile, there was no greater desire than to return to their homeland and rebuild the temple of the Lord that the Babylonians destroyed during their conquest in 587 BC.

Josh and I wanted nothing more than for him to return home and for our lives to return to normal. Both of us desired to break free from this hospital exile and begin rebuilding the parts of our lives that had broken. However, the closer we came to that reality, the more difficult it became to accept.

There was only One who could help ease that despair and claim the victory.

> *"But now, for a brief moment, the Lord our God*
> *has been gracious in leaving us a remnant*
> *and giving us a firm place in his sanctuary,*
> *and so our God gives light to our eyes*
> *and a little relief from our bondage."*
>
> *Ezra 9:8*

Tears streamed down the faces of the older Jews as they wandered the ruins of the city. Many of them had lived through the original destruction and captivity of their beloved Jerusalem. The younger Israelites born during the seventy years of bondage stared curiously at the unfamiliar surroundings with widened eyes. Some wondered if the four months of difficult travel and the separation from friends and family who refused to leave the comforts of Babylon were really worth it.

God had moved the king of Persia's heart to allow them to return and rebuild the temple of the Lord that had been completely demolished. The excitement of that task began to lose some of its gleam as the reality of what they now faced set in. They were merely fifty thousand strong and the only inhabitants currently living in the region of Judah. The massive rebuilding effort was going to take planning, organization, and focus. It was a daunting effort that must have seemed frustrating and impossible.

Within seven months, however, they were successful in rebuilding the altar on its original foundation and were able to begin sacrificing burnt offerings to the Lord. It was a cause for celebration to see the smoke drifting up from the altar each day. For those who had personally witnessed these daily sacrifices before the exile, it was a blessed reunion with the lives they once had. To them, the sweet aroma signified the ending of their bondage. They had completed this great feat in only a few months and many were satisfied. Standing as a group in front of the altar, they celebrated and rejoiced, their backs turned away from the ruins of the Lord's temple where not a single stone had been moved.

The altar was important. The sacrifices were a vital part of their faith, but it wasn't the task that had moved the heart of King Cyrus of Persia. God didn't move through Cyrus to allow the Jews to return and rebuild only the altar. The presence of God couldn't dwell in the altar. The temple must be rebuilt. The reservations and anxieties of the Jewish leaders needed to be overcome. They had to put aside their fears of neighboring enemies who set out to frustrate and discourage their efforts. They should have kept their focus on the promise that God had allowed them to return for a purpose and that His purposes would never fail.

Unfortunately, it would take the Jews seventeen additional years to accomplish that which God had commissioned them to complete. Seventeen years of discouragements, bribery of officials, accusations, and letter writing by their enemies to the King of Persia trying to convince him of their rebellious hearts. These same enemies successfully convinced the king that if the temple were to be fully rebuilt, all tribute and taxes paid to him by the Jewish people would end.

For the Jews who had faithfully returned to their beloved homeland, each time they passed by the temple whose walls and foundations showed only the slightest marks of improvements, their questions mounted. Why did God allow them to return if he wasn't going to help them rebuild? Why were they continually mocked and threatened by their neighbors if they were supposed to be God's chosen people? Why didn't they just stay in Babylon where their family members continued to thrive and prosper even if they remained in bondage?

Fifty-seven years later, after the temple was finally complete, another group of exiles returned to Jerusalem. Among them was a priest named Ezra. Through his faithfulness and obedience to God, Ezra was able to reform the new Jewish nation, teaching them about the law and their place in God's plan. It took seventeen years to complete the temple and decades following that for the Jews to realize that God's promises had never once failed. With Ezra's teaching, they were able to understand that despite all that had occurred, they were indeed God's chosen people.

The future before us was a tremendous weight that at times seemed unbearable. At face value, our circumstance certainly seemed overwhelming. Josh wouldn't be walking home as he'd hoped, and my fears threatened to destroy the foundation of faith I had worked so hard to build. Yet like the Jews who stood before the temple of the Lord in Jerusalem listening to the teaching of Ezra, the more we turned our hearts back toward the Lord, the more we began to realize our place in His glorious plan. We could rest in the blessed assurance that those plans would never fail.

We had to remain faithful, even if it took us another seventeen years.

NINE

COMING HOME

"But while he was still a long way off, his father saw him and was filled with compassion for him; he ran to his son, threw his arms around him, and kissed him."

Luke 15:20

It was a Thursday. Seventy-two days had passed since Josh had been admitted to the hospital with a severe case of viral meningitis. He would finally be returning home. We had prayed about this day; had dreamed of what it would feel like for ten long weeks. Now it was finally here. I took a few extra moments that morning to convene with God before taking Jesi to school. I needed to be still and allow the Holy Spirit to fill my heart with peace and joy, and to cast all my fears and anxieties about the next chapter of our lives into God's open hands.

With an uplifted spirit, I embraced Jesi as we walked into the school, her excitement as palpable as the joy I felt within my own heart. She couldn't wait to tell her teacher and classmates the good news. I saw several of them celebrating with her and exchanging high-fives. No more travels across town after school; no more hastily eaten dinners and hospital toys to play with. No more tear-filled rides in our car after leaving Josh each evening. Although I fully understood that our challenges wouldn't end with his discharge, today was the day to forget the worry and simply celebrate.

Celebrate his homecoming.

Celebrate the progress he continued to make each day.

Celebrate the amazing and unending faithfulness of God.

Driving across town, I felt my heart flutter when I thought about how special the trip back would be that afternoon. I decided to let the tears flow this time without reserve. These precious moments alone in my car with God each day had become instrumental in the healing of my emotional roller coaster. There was just enough time to let God smooth out those peaks and valleys with his assurances before I entered through the hospital doors.

As I walked through the hospital parking lot, I let my senses take over so I could mentally record every detail of this day. The crisp autumn air was refreshing. The warming glow of the sun swaddled me like a blanket. Soft, fluffy clouds drifted gently in the blue skies above. I heard the birds chirping happily in the trees that lined the road next to the building.

Their songs of joy reminded me of Psalms 28:7. "The Lord is my strength and my shield; my heart trusts in him, and he helps me. My heart leaps for joy, and with my song I praise him." This scripture had encouraged me countless times over the past three months during those moments of extreme loneliness. Reaching the double doors of the entrance, I paused briefly to close my eyes and lift one more prayer heavenward. No matter what, I knew that God would hold this day, and us, in His hands.

"I can't believe it. We finally made it!" Josh's mom walked over and embraced me with a bear hug as I entered his room.

"Neither of us could sleep last night, we were so excited. We decided to get up early and come to the hospital as soon as we could," my father-in-law confessed as he handed over a large iced coffee to me. He smiled. "We brought your favorite."

"Hey you." I set my coffee down and wrapped my arms around Josh's shoulders. He was sitting up in his armchair, fully dressed and ready to leave.

"Let's just leave right now," he joked.

"We can't leave just yet, you still have to try to walk, remember?" I smiled at my rhetorical question. Josh didn't need a reminder that he would be attempting to take a few steps this morning; it was all he had been talking about for days.

We spent the next hour sitting in Josh's room, anticipating the final session of physical therapy scheduled this morning. Josh would be released after lunch when all his discharge paperwork was complete. While he wasn't going to walk out of the hospital today, his therapists wanted to see if he would be able to take a few steps on his own before he left. Nervous for him, I understood how important this was to his overall progress.

All four of us made our way to the section of the rehab gym that housed the parallel bars. Josh hadn't yet had the strength to stand up long enough to use them, but it was his goal to try today. My hands shook in excitement while I attempted to steady my phone and record the next few minutes in pictures. Josh's face was set in gridlocked determination as three of his therapists surrounded him for support.

They encouraged him to take a few deep breaths and take his time before trying to stand up.

My heart lurched when I saw Josh let go of the wheelchair arms and push his body upward. In immediate response, two of his therapists grabbed both sides of his waist belt to help support him. One more therapist stood directly behind him positioning the wheelchair against the back of his legs in case he became fatigued. I swelled with pride as he labored through every step, grasping tightly to the bars for support. Three steps later, he collapsed into his chair, sweat plastered on his forehead, his face covered with an enormous grin. I threw my phone down and ran over to embrace him, my tears of joy drenching the top of his head.

"You did it! I am so incredibly proud of you." I hugged Josh once more before everyone else who wanted to congratulate him invaded our space.

It was a momentous occasion, and our family—Josh, his parents, and I—celebrated this incredible accomplishment with everyone in the room. This was tangible proof that Josh's body was indeed recovering, despite the agonizingly slow healing process. It was proof of the hope that we professed, and while it wasn't exactly what we had envisioned for this day, it was more than enough for all of us.

After he was finished with his therapy session, Josh's parents left to finish the final preparations at our house and to meet my parents, who would be joining us later for the homecoming. It was now time for Josh and me to start saying our good-byes to the hospital staff. These nurses and therapists had helped us through some of our toughest days; witnessing all the highs and lows. They had become our friends and we would dearly miss their support and encouragement.

"We wish you the very best on your recovery," his recreational therapist said.

"I'm so happy for you!" Josh's occupational therapist exclaimed.

"We are extremely proud of you, Josh," said Kristi. "You have been an inspiration to all of us during your time here." Kristi presented Josh with a laminated card that held a small four-leaf clover inside. "Good luck." She wiped her face after giving both of us hugs.

As we exchanged hugs and laughter, we did our best to keep the moment lighthearted and memorable. Almost every person we encountered as we continued down the hallway past the nurses' station offered similar sentiments. Even those who had never attended to Josh directly were affected either by his story or by his infectious determination to get better.

Returning to his room, I finished gathering up two bags of clothes, his Bible, and a fishing book he received as a birthday present back in August. All that remained now was to wait for his doctor to complete his discharge instructions and hand over his final paperwork and prescription. We took a few quiet moments to hold hands and pray together in his room. Finally, we had our release approval.

Josh could go home.

Returning down the same hallway we had traveled numerous times before, Josh and I now completed our final journey toward the parking lot. I had purposefully parked our car in the lot farthest away from his room in order for us to say our good-byes. We had kept his former nurse, Robert, informed of his discharge date and he requested to join us as we left. We passed by the courtyard where we had spent many weekend afternoons soaking in the sunshine. We paused for a minute as I wheeled Josh through the rehab gym where he had spent three hours each day of the last four weeks. On our way toward the exterior doors, we passed by the transitional care unit where Josh's nerves had finally started coming back to life.

"Take care of yourself, and be sure to come back and visit us soon!" One of the registered nurses who attended to Josh during his stay in TCU said. She stood up from behind the nurses' station desk, walked around the corner, and leaned down to give Josh a hug.

She pointed toward the direction of the exterior doors, only a few feet away from the desk. "I know that you wanted to walk out those doors when you left, but just remember how far you have come in such a short time. Don't lose sight of that." She gave his shoulder one last squeeze and then walked over to hold the door open for Josh's chair to pass through.

We were met by the bright light of the afternoon sun as the hospital doors closed behind us. Robert stayed and helped transfer Josh from his wheelchair into the car. I remained outside to learn how to secure the wheelchair into the car's trunk; a task that I would repeat many times over the next year. Now it was time to say our final good-bye.

"You be good, buddy." Robert leaned into the open passenger side door and reached out for Josh's hand. With a firm shake, he signaled it was now time for us to leave.

"Good-bye, Robert," I said. "Thank you so much for all of your support and encouragement. It's meant a lot to both of us." I gave him a hug and then climbed into the driver's seat of my car.

For the first few minutes neither of us could speak. I had traveled down these same streets for seventy-two straight days, hoping and praying for the day when Josh would ride in the car with me. Now that my wish finally came true, I was speechless. Josh was the first to interrupt the silence, his voice trembling in disbelief.

"This is really happening, isn't it?" he asked. I reached over and squeezed his hand, fighting tears once more.

"I can hardly believe it myself. It still doesn't seem real," I replied, keeping my eyes on the road.

Our anticipation heightened the closer we came to our house. I drove slowly down the street toward the house, allowing Josh a few quiet minutes to absorb the sights and sounds of our neighborhood. As I turned into our driveway, the celebration began in earnest. Jesi bounded down the street, my mother-in-law following close behind. What better present for a five-year-old than to get out of school and discover that her father, who'd been hospitalized for three months, had finally returned home?

The next few seconds were a whirlwind of emotions. My parents, who had arrived in town earlier in the day, emerged from our house along with my father-in law, greeting both of us with hugs and tears of joy. My dad walked over to our car and offered to help me transfer Josh into his wheelchair and push him up our newly installed wheelchair ramp. After we lifted the wheels of his chair up and over the threshold of our home, Josh immediately called our dogs over to him, a sound that I hadn't heard since that fateful day in July. None of us would ever forget the answer Josh received.

I heard the noise before I realized what was happening. As my dad wheeled Josh into our living room, our dog, Jake, responded to his call with the most unexpected reaction. It wasn't a bark, or a squeal; our dog was crying. Jake jumped up into Josh's lap and remained there for several minutes, pressed up against his chest, licking his face and arms in an act of exuberant love. There wasn't a dry eye in the room as each of us witnessed this dramatic reunion between two best friends.

Once again, God was using the unusual and extraordinary to demonstrate His unending faithfulness and amazing love.

Late that night after our extended families had gone home and both Josh and Jesi had fallen asleep in exhaustion over the day's events, I took advantage of the quietness in the house to review my Bible reading for the day. I had kept this one separated from the rest for a very special reason. This night, I needed to reflect on a beautiful story of redemption and the celebration of a much-awaited homecoming. I opened my Bible to the book of Luke and let the story of the prodigal son returning home fill my heart with hope.

> *"Let's have a feast and celebrate.*
> *For this son of mine was dead and is alive again;*
> *he was lost and is found."*
>
> *Luke 15:23–24*

> *The father stood alone at the edge of his front porch. Clouds dotted the sky above as a soft wind caressed the tops of the trees. It was a beautiful day; however, he was unable to enjoy it. His heart still mourned for the son he had lost; the son who had demanded his share of the inheritance and left many months ago. Regardless of the events that had led to the departure, he could still be found in front of his house daily, staring out across the fields in hopes that the form of his son would soon appear in the distance.*

Ignoring the chastisement from other family members, he believed deep down that his son would one day come home. He had long since forgiven the bitter words spoken that fateful day, and prayed that in time his wife and remaining son would be able to forgive as well. His life would never be the same until his family was whole again.

The clouds drifted sluggishly across the sky and the slight breeze had disappeared. Turning his body back toward the house, the father's shoulders heaved with another sigh of disappointment. Then, he heard an unusual sound that began as a faint whisper but quickly increased in volume. Looking around his property in search of where this peculiar noise originated from, he noticed something glimmer in the distance across the field from the house. Blinking several times, he rubbed his eyes to ensure that his mind wasn't being tricked by the brightness of the sun.

This time, there was no deceit involved. A form began to emerge from the glimmer. The faint whisper developed into syllables of words. Even from far away he recognized the lilt of the voice. Overwhelming compassion and joy filled his heart as he began to run across the field toward his son.

He was home.

His son had returned.

Nothing else mattered. Nothing else could fill his heart with such joy. The memories of past hurt and anger vanished as the two men finally closed the gap between them and embraced. The moment seemed to last forever. Tears streaming down their faces and arms locked around each other, neither wanted to be the first to let go. When they finally did separate, it was only for a few inches. With his father's arm wrapped around his shoulder, the son walked slowly back toward the house, wiping away the tears that continued to pour down his face.

During their embrace the son pleaded for forgiveness from his father, apologizing for the grievance brought upon his family by his actions and accepting the fact that he might not be welcomed back in as a son. Though he had done nothing but ask for forgiveness, he watched as his father rushed through the house, gathering servants and requesting that the best of his livestock be prepared for the feast. There was to be a massive celebration.

The prodigal son is one of the most well-known stories in the Bible. The son made the choice to leave his family; Josh did not. While their journeys took them down different paths, neither felt like they would ever be able to return back home and to the life they once knew. The prodigal son feared the rejection and resentment upon his return. Josh feared that his body might never fully recover from this disease and that his life might never be the same. Both desired to go home; both were unsure of what their futures would hold.

Jesus used the story of the prodigal son to describe the depth of the love God has for us. As our Heavenly Father, God will never stop scanning the horizon for our return, and the kingdom of heaven will never stop celebrating when those who are lost have finally come home. God was indeed celebrating with us this day. Josh had finally come home.

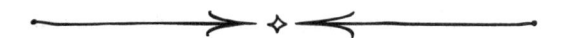

I fumbled nervously through the large box of gauze, bandages, tape, cream, and an assortment of other medical supplies delivered to our home the day before. I desperately tried to recall the exact order of wound-dressing steps that Josh's skin doctor had reviewed with me yesterday, but my hands shook as I looked at the items laid out before me on the bed. It was very important that I follow the precise instructions on dressing and cleaning his bedsore. Healing of this wound was imperative. Josh's skin doctor wouldn't release him to begin outpatient therapy until he was satisfied the bedsore had closed up enough to safely begin exercising.

Praying that I had completed the task correctly, I informed Josh that I was finished, leaning over to give him a quick hug of encouragement. Even with all my emotional and mental preparations for Josh's homecoming, I hadn't completely comprehended the scope of my new responsibilities. In the rush of excitement to ensure that everything was ready for him to come home, I had neglected to prepare the most important part: my own heart.

When Josh was away, our home had become a sanctuary for me, a safe haven away from the stresses and anxieties of hospital life. It was a place where I could experience the emotional breakdowns and spiritual breakthroughs necessary for me to make it through each difficult situation. Jesi and I had created new daily routines to retain a semblance of normalcy in our lives. She coveted those precious moments each evening when we would go to bed at the same time, calling Josh to tell him good night and then singing or talking about what she learned at school that day before falling asleep. I was used to waking up at a certain time to get both of us ready for work and school.

Now, through no fault of Josh's or anyone else, everything was different. Besides getting myself ready, mornings now included cleaning and changing the bandages of Josh's bedsore, helping him get up and dressed, feeding and watering our animals, and making sure that Jesi was ready for school. Our sleep patterns at night weren't the same either. Josh would need help late at night, forced to call my phone to wake me up because Jesi and I slept upstairs and couldn't hear if he cried out. These calls would sometimes repeat themselves as I struggled to wake up from a deep sleep and make my way downstairs to help him.

Household chores pulled at me, too. I hadn't cooked a meal in months. Meal preparation and food supplies required shopping time at the grocery store. Every minute spent away from the house intensified my guilt, as I knew that Josh needed me there for both physical and emotional support and strength. After working all day and coming home to cook dinner and assist Josh with his needs, I had very little energy left for cleaning or laundry.

For Josh, the most difficult challenge was accepting that his old established routines at the hospital were now gone. There was no instant-response nurse call button; no therapy sessions and no company during the day. His physical restrictions limited him to only a few rooms in the downstairs of our house. From bed to wheelchair, from wheelchair to recliner, and then back to bed. Repeat. Josh spent most of his time now watching television or thinking about his situation. My dad had arranged to come stay with him twice a week, and there were weekly visits from the home-health nurse, but for the majority of the day he was alone.

Jesi continued to display her childlike enthusiasm about Josh being home and gratefulness that we no longer had to go to the hospital to visit him, but I knew that deep down, the stress of seeing him in his current condition had to be bothering her. She would cling to me as I lay down with her each night, not allowing me to move until she fell asleep. She held my hand tightly while walking into school each morning, letting go only when she saw her friends wave to her from their place in line. A few days before, while picking up toys in her room, I found a drawing she had made of our family; her small form standing next to me while Josh sat in a wheelchair on the other side of us.

Everything had changed.

My breakdowns were now limited to the time spent in my car on my morning and evening work commute. Through my tears and my prayers, the Holy Spirit would intervene and provide me with the strength to endure. I wanted to be strong enough for my family. I wanted to be the provider and meet all their needs, but there were days when I felt that I had fallen hopelessly short of their expectations. The weight of this transition was intense.

Since I had very little free time at night for my Bible readings, I began using my lunch hour as a means to finish reviewing the scriptures I had left on my list. Today's story, about Noah, was located in the book of Genesis. It took Noah one hundred years to build the ark. Despite an entire generation of ridicule and rejection from his friends and neighbors, he remained faithful and obedient to God's instructions. From the moment that the Lord sealed the great door of the ark and the floodgates of heaven opened, Noah's life would never be the same.

It could never be the same again.

"Then God said to Noah and to his sons with him:
I now establish my covenant with you
And with your descendants after you."

Genesis 9:8

All he could see was rain. Noah stood alone under the beams of the ark's roof, looking out through the opening he had built to the world below. A thick covering of dark clouds above produced massive amounts of rain that mercilessly pelted the roof and sides of the ark. It had only been a few days, but the ground below the massive boat had already started to fill with water and Noah could hear the creaking of the ark's support beams as they shifted in the increasing water flow. It wouldn't be much longer until these beams would fall away from the ark. The colossal vessel would slowly drift past the forest whose trees had provided the timber.

In the back of his mind, Noah could still hear the voices of his friends and neighbors mocking his building efforts at every turn. Despite their harsh words, tears streamed down his face, knowing that they would perish as the floodwaters continued to rise. In fact, every living thing on earth would perish except for the animals God had instructed Noah and his family to care for. From the very first direction God had given him months ago, he had obeyed all of them to the letter. He had done all that the Lord commanded, and believed implicitly in the will of God, yet he still found himself grieving for the world he was losing.

Turning at the sound of his son Shem's voice from the deck below, Noah knew feeding-time duties awaited him as he climbed back down the ladder. He was greeted by the bleats and chirps and snorts of the various animals sheltered within the walls of the massive boat. A calming warmth radiated from the different groups of animals as he passed by each one. One pair, a male and a female of each species, had been preserved on the ark.

When he reached the pair of horses stabled next to the cows, he paused a brief moment and stood in front of their gate, allowing the curious animals to sniff at his hair and face. The male horse leaned over and nuzzled the side of his neck in a comforting display of affection. Noah closed his eyes for a moment and allowed these innocent animals to soothe away a piece of the grief he continued to bear.

For forty days and nights, the floodwaters would continue to rise. Each morning Noah would make his way to the opening in the roof and look to the mountain ridges in the east. As the days passed, he could see less of them, until one day they were simply gone. The ark and its inhabitants were the only living things remaining on the earth, floating in watery suspension above the world for over six months. It would take six more months after that for the water to recede and the earth below to become inhabitable once more.

Patience and willingness to be faithful to God's plans for his life defined the last few years of Noah's life. He didn't know the ending to his story. He trusted and believed that God had spared his life and that of his family for a reason, but what would happen when the floodwaters finally receded? What would this new world be like, and would he always be haunted by the memories of those who had been lost?

For Noah, everything had changed.

So much was different for Josh and me as we began our transition into the new order of our lives. Our flood of pain and grief had threatened to bury us at first as we navigated through the medical unknowns. Now that we had finally returned to our own solid ground, it truly did feel like a new beginning for both of us, in so many ways. How we would endure and make it through the months and years to come was an unknown, best left in the hands of God.

Like Noah taking that first step off that great boat after they had settled onto dry land, we had to believe and trust in the plans God had for us. He had been faithful to provide for us through every twist and turn of our journey thus far. We had no reason to believe that what lay ahead of us would be any different.

God be praised, we would survive.

From the Eyes of a Five-Year-Old

Jesi's Perspective

My daddy got a headache one day when he went on a camping trip. I think a mosquito bit him. When he came home, we called an ambulance and he went to the hospital. I was so, so sad. I stayed with my Grandpa Roger for the first few days. It was fun, but I missed my family.

It made me mad that Daddy got sick and I was mad at whatever gave him the headache. I was also sad because when you see somebody you love hurting, you don't want them to get hurt. I missed him so much. Sometimes, before I went to sleep, I used to think of him and cry in the bed.

I didn't really understand that he was paralyzed and that he wasn't going to be able to use his legs for so long. It was hard to see him like that. I looked forward to going to the hospital every day to visit him and eat pizza from Subway with my mom.

The day Daddy was coming home from the hospital, I was so excited! I jumped up and down in bare feet and I was so glad. I couldn't wait to see him. I remember our dog, Jake, was the most excited to see him; he was moaning and barking and jumping up in the front window of our house.

I was disappointed when he came home and wasn't able to do all the things he used to do. I felt bad for him. I felt sad when he thought he hurt my feelings but he actually didn't. It was fun being able to go to his therapy with him and help him out a few times. The people there were nice and let me play in the gym while Daddy was doing his workouts.

God helped my daddy get better every day. God helped him recognize that he wasn't alone and that we were always with him.

TEN

LOOKING UP INTO THE LIGHT

"He said, 'Look! I see four men walking around in the fire, unbound and unharmed, and the fourth looks like a son of the gods.'"

Daniel 3:25

My heart fluttered nervously as I closed the car door behind Josh and awkwardly maneuvered his heavy wheelchair into the trunk. An appointment scheduled with Josh's family doctor was our first adventure together out into the world after his discharge and we were both anxious. I had done my best to allow enough time to make it across town through midmorning traffic, but setbacks at the house had postponed our departure. Added to everything was Josh's anxiety about interactions with the public after three months of hospital confinement. Few words were exchanged between us as I drove across town.

We pulled into the doctor's office parking lot an hour later, right at our scheduled appointment time, after seeming to catch every red light. Hustling as quickly as I could, I opened the trunk to my car and pulled out the wheelchair. It took a few minutes to get Josh transferred over, and I was nervous about our already-late arrival time. Simultaneously walking and pushing his wheelchair down the hallway toward the elevators at a fast pace, I prayed the delay wouldn't cause us to lose our scheduled appointment with his doctor. One look at the receptionist's sour face when we entered the doctor's office told us differently.

"You were supposed to be here fifteen minutes ago. There's nothing we can do."

Fighting back tears of frustration, I tried to explain to her the reasons for our late arrival, but instead of kindness or compassion, we were met with only a blank stare. After she remained silent and didn't offer to reschedule our appointment, I turned Josh's wheelchair back around and headed back out the door of their office. This was the first time I was solely responsible for getting Josh around town to one of his appointments, and I felt like I had failed miserably. I apologized to him multiple times as I pushed his wheelchair back down the hallway toward the parking garage.

"It's not your fault, Maggie," Josh repeated several times. "You did everything you could. There was no reason for them to act that way."

Two days later, we had an appointment scheduled with Josh's wound care doctor regarding his bedsore. This was a checkup that we couldn't afford to miss. Arriving fifteen minutes early, I pushed Josh's chair up to the receptionist's window to report our presence. We were both put at ease by the receptionist's friendly demeanor; however, those hopes were dashed when we noticed her smile quickly turn to a frown. Once more, I had failed. She informed us that we should have been there an hour prior to fill out the necessary paperwork. I closed my eyes and said a prayer that I wouldn't respond back to her with a frustrated attitude.

Apologizing profusely, I explained that the discharge nurse at the hospital hadn't provided us with specific instructions about these appointments, only dates and times. Thankfully, my justifications were met with kindness this time as she handed over a clipboard full of paperwork and suggested I find a seat to begin filling it out.

We left their office several hours later, encouraged by the words of his doctor. The bedsore appeared to be healing at a faster rate than when Josh was in the hospital. He guaranteed us that once it had fully healed, Josh would be able to begin outpatient therapy. However, even with the rapid healing, it would still be several more weeks before the doctor could release us from his care. As disappointing as this news was, we reassured ourselves that Josh was still making progress, even if these periods of waiting were difficult to bear.

The struggles continued. We faced situations where mercy and compassion, or the lack of it, were emphasized as never before. There were the times when we needed to use the disabled parking spaces at the doctor's office and we discovered people were using them without handicap permits or licenses. There were the instances when I attempted to maneuver Josh's wheelchair through a closed doorway, balancing the door with my hip as I opened it, while other people walked right by us without even a glance or an offer to help.

Josh's paralysis wasn't permanent, but he would be required to use his wheelchair until his body became strong enough to support his full weight. It was hard enough for us to make this transition and accept the fact Josh would be wheelchair bound for months; harder still to witness those moments where others couldn't see past his disability. However, not everyone was unkind. We did encounter people who offered to hold the door for me as I pushed Josh's wheelchair through, people who didn't stare at us in revulsion, but smiled at us cheerfully while asking if we needed any help. These encouraging acts of kindness from strangers smoothed over the obvious lack of compassion and empathy by others.

For the first few weeks, Josh didn't leave the house at all, except for his weekly wound care doctor appointments. After three months of isolation from what used to be normal life for us, we decided to be brave and venture out one evening. The one thing Josh wasn't limited in doing was going out to eat. Almost all restaurants provide handicap-accessible entrances and wheelchair ramps. I suggested we eat at our favorite Mexican restaurant, El Maguey, a place I had hoped wouldn't be very crowded during a weekday dinnertime.

My proposal—meant to help take Josh's mind off current frustrations—felt like yet another failure as I pulled into one of the only empty spaces left in the parking lot. While I pushed his wheelchair up the ramp in front of the building, scores of college-aged young adults poured in around us. I sensed the tension in Josh's body increase as we waited in line for a table, and I tried not to dwell on the sideways glances in our direction.

A wave of relief washed over me as a young server motioned toward us, quickly navigating Josh and me through the crowd to an open table. With kindness and genuine compassion, she helped move chairs around to make room for his wheelchair. Securely tucking his chair underneath the table, I sat down across from him.

"What sounds good to you?" I asked Josh while browsing the menu. "Are you going to get your usual king burrito or go for the chori pollo tonight?"

The waiter approached the table. "Better bring an extra bowl of chips for us tonight," I suggested with a smile.

Despite the stress and embarrassment of the earlier glances, we did our best to enjoy the moment for what it was, finding a sense of normalcy while we discussed what food to order. The kindness of the restaurant staff hadn't been lost on either of us. An evening that could have been filled with negative emotions was redirected by a simple act of selflessness.

This restaurant outing provided Josh with enough confidence to make another social appearance, this time for church the following Sunday. I was overjoyed that he wanted to join Jesi and me, as I knew how desperately all three of us could use the encouragement of a worship service. Nothing could shift my attitude and perspective more than the reassurances that lay within the lyrics and chords of praise music.

Sunday morning brought air that was crisp and cold, with a light fluttering of snow falling from the sky. The snowflakes began to cover the ground in a beautiful white blanket. It was sign of renewal and fresh beginnings. For me, it represented how God takes the pain and sadness of life and makes it white as snow. The heartache of our transition had been threatening to undo the joy and happiness of Josh's return home. All three of us were in need of another reminder of the faithfulness of God.

Our pastor and his wife, along with several other couples that had visited Josh in the hospital, greeted us upon our arrival at front doors of the church.

Looking Up into the Light

"It's so good to see you, Josh!"

"Wow, what an answer to prayer, seeing you sitting up in your chair like that!" another member of our church chimed in. She was one of many "prayer warriors" who had kept us encouraged and loved.

"Thank you so much for all your support." I embraced each of them with a heart full of emotions, remembering the days when I had felt the encouragement of those very prayers.

Entering the auditorium, I located a good spot for us to sit together, allowing room for his wheelchair. I held his hand as I sang along with the worship songs, my heart full of emotions. In only a matter of months, our lives had been uprooted and radically shifted in the opposite direction. Nothing would ever be the same and I began to recognize that it truly never could. The Holy Spirit had touched our lives. Everything we did from this point forward should be a reflection of that spiritual contact.

I waited until late that night after everyone else was asleep to read over my daily Bible verse selection. Hezekiah, who reigned as king of Judah seven hundred years before the birth of Christ, had always been one of my favorite characters from the Bible. Several years ago, I had read a series of fictional books by the author Lynn Austin about Hezekiah's life that I found inspirational. The reading tonight was equally inspiring as I reflected on the story of the prideful Assyrian army that claimed they would demolish the city of Jerusalem and take its' inhabitants captive.

Despite the imminent threat of 185,000 Assyrian soldiers surrounding the city, God had a plan for the kingdom of Judah and for Jerusalem herself. They would be spared, for a time. While Hezekiah lay praying on the floor of the temple, clothed in sackcloth and anguish, his request was not just for his nation to be saved. He prayed that this particular defeat, which could only come from a supernatural source, would be a sign to all kingdoms of the earth that there was only one, true God.

> *"Then will the eyes of the blind be opened*
> *and the ears of the deaf unstopped.*
> *Then will the lame leap like a deer,*
> *and the mute tongue shout for joy."*
>
> *Isaiah 35:5–6*

The hem of King Hezekiah's sackcloth brushed against the golden-paneled wood floor beneath his feet. The king wasn't surprised to find the temple empty of priests this morning as they had been instructed to fast and pray in their own chambers. It was possible that they were also taking shelter in the depths of the temple, fearful of the events occurring just outside the city gates. This same fear had prompted the King of Judah to tear his clothes in distress and replace them with garments woven from coarse goat's hair. The sackcloth was the traditional attire for the Jewish people when they were in mourning.

Today could qualify as a day of mourning for the inhabitants of Judah. King Sennacherib of Assyria had sent a large army of troops to Jerusalem. The Assyrian army was a brutal, ruthless enemy who left nothing but destruction in their wake. Smoke from the ashes of farms destroyed nearby was visible from the gates of the city. It was a terrifying, ominous sight for the people of

Jerusalem. Only the day before, Sennacherib had sent several of his officers to the gates of the city to deliver a message to Hezekiah and all the people living inside of the fortified city.

"Do you not know what I and my predecessors have done to all the people of the other lands? Were the gods of those nations ever able to deliver their land from my hand? How then can your god deliver you from my hand? Now, do not let Hezekiah deceive you and mislead you like this. Do not believe him, for no god of any nation or kingdom has been able to deliver his people from my hand or the hand of my predecessor!"

After the words were read, panic ensued. Desperate to assure his people they did not need to fear, King Hezekiah had requested that every person assemble in the square at the city gate. He waited patiently as they gathered before him, a great buzz of murmuring and anxiousness. They were scared, and rightfully so. Closing his eyes, he breathed a silent prayer for strength and confidence. God was on their side. His people needed to believe that, and they needed to see that he believed it as well. Raising his hand to silence the crowd, Hezekiah cleared his throat and began to speak. The words came out strong and clear, with a confident faithfulness.

"Be strong and courageous. Do not be afraid or discouraged because of the king of Assyria and the vast army with him, for there is a greater power with us than with him. With him is only the arm of flesh, but

with us is the Lord our God to help us and to fight our battles."

His final declaration hung in the air as the crowd cheered and praised God. They were reminded of the one true God and everything he had done for Israel and for the land of Judah. They trusted the words spoken by their king, and because of his faith, he was able to instill that same confidence within his people.

Their faith continued to prevail, despite the continuous psychological warfare flowing from the Assyrian camp. Day after day, they ridiculed God and mocked those who believed they would be spared. The Assyrian officers positioned outside the city gates hurled insults up at the Jewish soldiers and others who were keeping watch on top of the wall. They were confident that they could break the city by first breaking the spirit of the people. Unfortunately, their confidence was misplaced. Little did the Assyrian army know, but their lives hung in the balance.

God was about to answer the prayers of Hezekiah in a mighty way.

Fear was our Assyrian army, camped outside the gates of our hearts, ready to attack at a moment's notice. Fear of the transition. Fear of the pain that lived around every corner of Josh's recovery. Fear of what our lives were going to be like living in the aftermath of this disease, both economically and emotionally. Fear that we might not be strong enough to make it through this trial. It lied to us and manipulated our thoughts by whispering unimaginable scenarios in our ears. It wanted us to lose hope and believe that we would fail.

The only way to make it through this war was to have a faith so bold, so confident, and so certain, that nothing could shake it from its foundation. As we struggled through every battle, hope and faith became the shields encircling our family, protecting us at all angles. Like a solider trained in the ways of war, so was our entire experience fertile training ground for learning how to place our God in front of our fears.

We would walk in the confidence of King Hezekiah. Through the display of our faith, we could encourage others who crossed our paths. And just maybe, they would come to believe in God. Not because of anything we had done, but because of how God was working through our family.

Now that would be the ultimate victory.

The next morning we awoke to a winter wonderland, with snow outside blanketing the world in a soft shade of white. Lurking behind the natural beauty, however, was one more source of anxiety that I had to face. Pulling on my snow boots, I grabbed a shovel and a few bags of rock salt and headed toward the wheelchair ramp in front of our house. I was excited and nervous at the same time. Excited that we had finally been given approval for Josh to begin outpatient physical therapy; nervous about whether I would be able to get him to his scheduled appointment this morning safely and on time.

After all the snow had been cleared and I was satisfied with the amount of rock salt on the ramp, Josh and I started our journey outside. With only a minor amount of sliding, I was successful in reaching the end of the ramp without either of us, or his chair, ending up sideways in the snow. Breathing a sigh of relief, I helped him into the passenger seat of our car and then secured his chair in the trunk. Josh grinned from ear to hear, barely containing his enthusiasm as we slowly made our way down the street.

It had been over a month since his discharge from the hospital. Five weeks of stress-filled doctor's appointments and challenges of transitioning into our new lifestyle had brought with it more anxiety than celebration. Josh's recovery was happening very slowly, just as his neurologist had predicted. Frustration had set in full swing due to the lack of physical exercise and boredom of isolation at home, compounded with the snail-like rate of improvement. We needed some good news, soon.

Thankfully, we received that news two days ago when the doctor responsible for managing his bedsore released Josh from his care, a gesture that indicated Josh could begin physical therapy work again. Today, our entrance into the hospital wouldn't be riddled with fear and uncertainty, but with eagerness and optimism.

After traveling down multiple corridors we finally reached the therapy waiting room. I signed in with the receptionist, sat down in the chair next to Josh, and grasped his hand, saying a short prayer. Not really knowing what to expect, I prayed that this therapy would be similar to what he had received previously, and that his new therapist would be kind and compassionate.

"Josh Allen." Both of us looked up toward the doorway when we heard his name called.

"My name is Kim. It's really great to meet you both. I just need to ask you a few questions before we get started today." Josh's newest therapist introduced herself with a firm handshake and a warm, gentle smile.

As our conversation continued, I was put at ease by her calm demeanor. Apparently, Josh's rare medical condition had preceded his arrival and Kim freely admitted that she was intrigued by his case.

"I'm humbled to play a part in your journey to recovery," she confided.

The workout room in this new facility promised to be a place full of happy memories. This would be the room where Josh would learn how to balance himself and stand upright. He would learn how to walk up and down stairs, and eventually walk again. This progress would inspire not only our small family, but also the world outside who had been following and praying for us along our journey. After Kim had given us a brief tour, we left the building with hearts full of hope for this next phase of our lives. It felt so incredibly good.

Due to the fact that I had already missed a great deal of work while Josh was in the hospital, an arrangement had been made between his mother and me regarding transportation. She would take him to the majority of his therapy appointments, and I would fill in when she was unable. She promised to take pictures and videos during the sessions when I wasn't there, to help journal his progress.

I jealously watched the videos pour in on my phone. Josh's newfound determination to use every second of outpatient therapy to his advantage meant that his recovery was now increasing at a remarkable pace. I wanted to be there with him and witness these miraculous events firsthand, and was grateful when I had the opportunity to go with him. The emotional encouragement I received watching him stand up straight with hands holding tightly to the parallel bars had no equal. It was awe inspiring to see him slowly place one foot in front of the other, or stand up while holding his own croquet mallet. The weight of the world outside seemed to melt away each time I was able to attend the therapy sessions with him.

Yet, even more remarkable than witnessing his recovery was the blessing of sharing these stories of inspiration with those around us. I would share pictures, videos, and stories of Josh's progress with my colleagues at work, on Facebook with friends and family, at church, or with the cashier at the grocery store. Every time the response would be one of amazement and encouragement.

It was snowing the day I drove Josh to his first therapy session, and it was snowing yet again the next time I was able to attend. So much snow had fallen the past few weeks that the schools in town had already experienced several closings because of this accumulation. Jesi was ecstatic about this snow day and excited to be able to join us this time. She loved playing with the small stool the therapists used in the children's department. While she might have had other reasons for being there, I knew that any involvement in her father's process would provide important memories for her to reflect back on later in life.

Today's session would be no less disappointing. With arms shaking and his safety belt harnessed securely around his midsection, Josh's face was set in concentration as he took one step after another. The weight of his upper body bore down on his legs, causing them to tremble and shake, baby deer–like, as they fought to hold themselves upright. Two of Josh's therapists followed directly behind him with his wheelchair, allowing him to take a break as he needed.

His goal for this day was to make it down the full length of the parallel bars and back. I could see fatigue start to set in as he reached the end of the first trip, but I knew that he would push himself to make it back to where he began. It was moments such as these that allowed Josh to feel like he was able to contribute something toward his progress. So much else had been left to forces outside his control. These exercises were mentally, physically, and spiritually therapeutic for both of us.

The next morning at work, I relayed this story to my coworkers and sent multiple messages to friends and family members about Josh's latest progress; I was humbled yet again, by how God was using our story to inspire others. It was now time for us to begin concentrating on what could be, instead of what was. There was hope at the end of this tunnel, and even though we might stumble and fall at times, we continued to have faith that God would guide us through to the other side.

I used my lunch hour that day to review my selected Bible scripture from the book of Daniel. I had recently found so much hope and strength within the chapter of this book; I couldn't help but read over this amazing story multiple times, each time ending with chills and a sense of incredible encouragement. I was in awe of the amount of faith it took for those three men to stand before the mighty king of Babylon and declare that they would not bow down before his statue. God was with Shadrach, Meshach, and Abednego, just as He was with Josh, Jesi, and myself during our trials. Once more, He kept His promise that He would never leave our side.

"Then King Nebuchadnezzar leaped to his feet in amazement and asked his advisors, 'Weren't there three men that we tied up and threw into the fire?'"

Daniel 3:24

The music played and thousands of people dropped to their knees, prostrate before the mighty King of Babylon. Every nation and every language within the Babylonian Empire was represented by the masses thronged around the large golden statue. While the symphony of horns, flutes, lyres, pipes, and all kinds of music played their melodic choruses, the sea of provincial officials continued their adulation. Only three men remained standing. They dared to disobey the direct orders given by King Nebuchadnezzar. A rebuke of the king's order meant severe punishment and most likely death.

Shadrach, Meshach, and Abednego dared to place their lives in the hands of God.

Furious when he received this news, King Nebuchadnezzar slammed his fist down on the arm of his throne and demanded these insubordinate Jews be brought before him immediately. The three men were located kneeling down in the middle of their private room, holding hands and praying for guidance. Busting down their door with a swift kick, the king's guard burst into their room and ordered his soldiers to seize the three men kneeling on the floor before them.

Holding up their hands in peaceful surrender, the men allowed the guards to shackle their arms together and lead them roughly out the door and through the maze of passageways toward the throne room of the king. Men and women attired in beautiful silk robes with sashes of gold around their waists stared in disgust at the plainly clothed Jews who were being led into the throne room. Who did they think they were, disobeying the orders of the one person who could take their lives away from them with a snap of his finger?

Seated on his throne, the king gave each of them one last chance to bow down and worship him, thus rectifying their situation. If they bowed down, all would be forgiven. However, if they chose to remain standing, their fate would be sealed. They would be taken immediately to the blazing furnace located down the hill from the palace and thrown inside. No mercy, no second chances; only death awaited.

With heads held high and legs firmly locked into place, Shadrach, Meshach, and Abednego refused to bow down. The words they spoke next surprised everyone in the room.

"King Nebuchadnezzar, we do not need to defend ourselves before you in this matter. If we are thrown into the blazing furnace, the God we serve is able to deliver us from it, and he will deliver us from Your Majesty's hand. But even if he does not, we want you to know, Your Majesty, that we will not serve your gods or worship the image of gold you have set up."

Reacting to this blatant disobedience, murderous rage overtook the king and he ordered the men to be thrown immediately into the fire. He also ordered his guards to increase the heat of the furnace seven times hotter than normal. The flames were so hot that they claimed the lives of the soldiers responsible for placing the prisoners, bound and tied up, into the fire. The men glanced at each other as they witnessed the soldiers falling down around them, yet despite the heat, they felt strangely at peace. All they could see was red, orange, and white, yet they continued on into the fire until they were fully submerged.

Watching the flicker of flames, they felt no heat, only a strange pressure similar to the feeling of being underwater. They felt the presence of the Lord before they saw him. Suddenly, a brilliant white light replaced the orange and red colors of the fire. A form emerged from behind them and placed his hand on the men's shoulders, a smile glowing on his face.

Jesus was with them.

From outside the furnace and a safe distance away, King Nebuchadnezzar observed. He saw the soldiers die, saw the men enter the fire unscathed, and he was surprised to see the bright white light emerge from the depths of the furnace. He had personally witnessed only three men go into the fire; how was it possible that four of them could be in there now? How could they be walking around and completely unharmed? It was incomprehensible. Only one reason could explain what the king was seeing.

He shouted at the men to come out of the fire, running up to them in amazement. Not a single hair on their head had been touched by the flames, nor were their robes scorched. As the king stood next to the men, he noticed the most incredible thing of all—not even the smell of smoke clung to them. These men dared to defy their king and were willing to give up their lives rather than bow down, yet they did not die. They had faith and believed God would be faithful to them, either way the story ended. They were at peace with leaving this world.

However, they did not leave.

God was not finished with them yet.

The first few days Josh was in the hospital, we stood inside our own symbolic furnace while the flames burned brighter. We had no idea what was in store for us and neither of us could have predicted what would happen. The meningitis; the days in the intensive care unit; the paralysis, the diagnosis; the fear; the uncertainty; the pain; the breakdown of relationships; the loss of normalcy, and the new beginnings. As each new circumstance and situation threatened to unravel our faith, we could feel the pressure from the flames bearing down. At times, we didn't know how we'd make it through.

Yet, we never felt the heat. Not a single hair was singed and no aroma of smoke clung to our clothes. The fire wanted to burn us to the ground, but the flames were no match for the brilliant white light that surrounded us. While we prayed for healing and for answers, Jesus stood next to us with his hand on our shoulder, shielding us from the blaze. His promise was that no matter the outcome, we would never be alone.

We would make it out of this furnace and our lives would never be the same.

Going Home

Josh's Perspective

I still have the date of my discharge memorized. October 3. It was all I could think about. I had so many goals for my therapy. I really wanted to be able to walk back out the doors of the hospital, but unfortunately, that wouldn't happen. I wanted to take a few steps on the parallel bars before I left, and I was so happy when they told me I could do that on my last day.

Going home was surreal. I was looking forward to having my family back and seeing my dog, Jake. I couldn't wait to be able to eat good, home-cooked food again. When I finally got to the house, the celebrations were awesome and it was so wonderful to be with the people who had been cheering me on during my recovery. However, once the party had ended and everyone had left, I was scared. I couldn't walk or go up the stairs to my bedroom, so a temporary living space had been created for me downstairs. Honestly, it felt like I was in a stranger's house. Everything was different and I had to get used to a new reality, yet again.

I came home on a Thursday and the next day my wife went back to work and my daughter went back to school. I was alone once more. I had a severe bedsore from my days in the hospital and my legs hurt constantly. I couldn't do anything yet and was limited to sitting in a chair all day long. Family members took turns picking Jesi up from school and dropping her off at the house with me. I was very nervous about those hours I was alone with her. I worried that

I couldn't take care of her, or myself, if an emergency happened. Those first few weeks during the transition home were very tough physically and emotionally.

I was so glad when they approved me to begin my outpatient therapy. I looked forward to every minute of it and never missed an appointment. My new therapists quickly became part of my extended support network. They encouraged and supported me, literally, every step of the way. I was nervous when I began walking for real, but I was never scared.

It wasn't always easy, but I had to get better, for myself and for my family.

ELEVEN

THIS IS NOT THE END

"Then Jesus said, 'Did I not tell you that if you believe, you will see the glory of God?'"

John 11:40

Light flickered from our Christmas tree as we watched our overjoyed five-year-old rip through her presents. Today was a day to look beyond transitions and disabilities and celebrate the blessing of being together again. I glanced over at Josh as Jesi continued to open her presents and saw that his tears mirrored my own. For me, there was no greater gift than having him once more by my side.

I was also excited because Josh had set a goal for himself to walk up the thirteen stairs in our house to the second floor on Christmas day. Five months had passed since he'd been in the upstairs section of our home. I worried that the strength required for him to tackle the stairs would cause his body too much stress, but I was thrilled that he had the desire to conquer them today.

I thought back to his therapy session only a few days before when he had stood up from his wheelchair and walked up a small set of stairs. Most of his work lately related to balance and being able to stand up straight and take a few steps at a time. Shuffling his feet was one thing; lifting his legs up in the air while maintaining his balance was quite another. In order to step up onto the stairs, the core of his body had to be strong enough.

I watched that day as he used the wooden railings on the stairs for upper body support, and labored a step at a time until reaching the middle platform. Taking a short break, he started forward to step back down four more stairs until reaching the floor and sinking into his wheelchair in exhaustion. It was an amazingly inspirational scene to witness.

Today, after Jesi had finished opening up her presents, Josh would be climbing up twice the number of stairs he did in therapy, with no place to take a break. To say I was nervous for him was an understatement, and I prayed that the newly installed hand railings would be strong enough to support him. After ensuring that his walker was located at the top of the stairs, I stood behind him for support, holding tightly to the belt secured around his waist. Gradually, Josh ascended each stair. When he reached the last step at the top, he immediately grasped ahold of his walker and looked down toward us, an enormous grin covering his face.

"You did it, Daddy!" Jesi exclaimed proudly.

"That was the best Christmas present ever!" I leaned over and hugged Josh's parents, wiping away the tears of joy.

The doctors had never been able to give us an official timetable for his full recovery. As the months passed, we realized that it was probably going to take a lot longer than the six months to a year predicted in Josh's original diagnosis, but we could never give up hope. Moments like these were the fuel that kept our hopes and dreams alive. We watched as he made progress, literally one step at a time.

I was unable to attend the next few therapy sessions, but the videos kept rolling in as promised. Josh began taking a few steps around the therapy room using only his walker for support. As his body became more stable, he was able to stand up for longer periods. He had finally reached a point where his therapists wanted him to begin walking, outside of the parallel bars. Three months ago, on the day he left the hospital, he took his first step. Now he would be walking. I knew how much this meant to Josh, how he struggled through the pain and fought for every step he took. These steps were representations of the hope we professed; manifestations of the glory of God creating beauty from our ashes.

That beauty began to present itself in some amazing ways. As I shared videos on Facebook and continued writing on my blog, I realized just how inspirational our story truly was. The more I shared, the more people would approach me in person or on social media, telling me how encouraged and inspired they were by Josh's progress. My honesty was opening the door for others to feel comfortable in sharing their own story of heartache, disappointment, or loss.

God was transforming our story into a beautiful narrative of hope. A few days after Christmas during my nightly quiet time, I opened my Bible to the book of Luke. Tonight's story was one of curiosity, heartache and miracles. One king, two sisters, and one brother were characters in a series of events that foreshadowed the death, burial, and resurrection of Jesus. Lazarus would die; Mary and Martha would grieve; Herod would become curious about Jesus; and Jesus would amaze them all.

"But Herod said, 'I beheaded John. Who then, is this I hear such things about?' And he tried to see him."

Luke 9:8

Gossip was nothing new to Herod's court. In fact, his courtiers thrived on the latest news, always wanting to be the first to inform their king. King Herod was devious and manipulative, and those living or working in his court had adapted to his thirst for information. The latest gossip revolved around the strange healer and his small band of followers who were roaming from town to town performing what people were calling miracles.

Little was known about the man himself, where he came from or what his intentions were. Some speculated that he meant no harm; that he was merely helping the poor and the sick. Others believed he might have motives that were more sinister. Those closest to Herod understood his deepest fears that the man might be trying to claim the throne. As the stories spread, so did Herod's anxiety. People were whispering that the Prophet Elijah must have returned, or that John the Baptist, whom Herod had personally beheaded, had been raised from the dead.

So much gossip. Herod had to see this man in person to determine if he was truly a threat. Despite several attempts to bring him in, the man failed to make an appearance. Herod would be left wondering about this curious person a little while longer. Jesus had more work to do.

Sometime later, Jesus would receive an urgent note from two of his followers who lived in the town of Bethany. The sisters were worried. Their brother hadn't eaten in days and had recently began coughing up blood. His body was pale and weakened to the point of death. Mary and Martha saw no other option but to send word to Jesus to come as quickly as he could. They believed Lazarus didn't have much time left.

Their request came with complications, however. If Jesus were to travel back to Judea, news would surely spread of his arrival and the Pharisees would send out soldiers to arrest him. They didn't believe in his claim that he was the Son of God and the savior of the Jews. They were afraid of his popularity and his apparent disregard of their authority. They wanted him dead. If Jesus were to be spotted in the regions close to Jerusalem, it wouldn't end well.

Despite this threat to his personal safety, his knowledge of future events and love for Lazarus and his family prompted his arrival at their home a few days later. As he walked down the path toward their home, Martha came to greet him, clothed in sadness and despair. While Jesus tarried in his travel plans, Lazarus had passed away. The sisters berated Jesus for his late arrival, confident that if he had been present their brother wouldn't have died. They couldn't have known, nor understood the significance of what was about to happen. Only Jesus could comprehend how the glory of God would shine through this moment in time.

Mary and Martha followed behind Jesus as they approached the tomb where the body of their brother had been laid to rest. Wiping away the tears he had just shed for his beloved friend, Jesus requested the stone in front of the tomb be rolled away. Confused by his instructions, Martha tried to dissuade him. Even though they had professed their faith in Jesus earlier, the sisters still didn't understand what was happening.

After a brief prayer, Jesus stood before the entrance to the tomb and called out in a loud, commanding voice, "Lazarus, come out!" The cry startled everyone within hearing distance. Lazarus's sisters glanced at each other in amazement and confusion. Suddenly, a form clothed in white appeared in the entrance to the tomb and began walking toward Jesus. Gasping for breath, Martha watched as the man unraveled the linen from around his face.

It was Lazarus.

He was alive.

Not long after, Herod would finally be granted the audience he had so desperately sought. Expecting Jesus to profess his authority as the Son of God by performing miracles, Herod and his soldiers plied him with questions and mocked him when he gave no replies. Herod didn't understand why Jesus kept silent and said nothing in his defense, even during the ridicule and scorn. After having his fun, Herod would return Jesus back to Pilate and the Jewish authorities. The only person who understood how this story would end was the man who stood in silence.

As we journeyed down the road of recovery, there were many times we found ourselves wondering why Jesus seemed to remain silent to our questions, knowing he was the only one that could provide the answers we sought. Yet, just when we felt consumed with the burdens of pain and sorrow, then would we hear the commanding voice of our Savior crying out to us.

"Children, come out!"

Jesus was beckoning us to come out from behind the ashes and into the glorious future he had planned for us.

Josh continued to progress at a rapid rate. Every session of therapy helped strengthen the core of his body, improving his balance and stability. He began to take steps by lifting his feet up rather than shuffling them on the floor. Because his balance was improving, he was able to begin walking without the use of his walker. Kim and his other therapists recognized that Josh had less than two months left before his sessions would end, and they did their best to utilize what time they had as effectively as they could.

On the next day I was able to attend therapy with him, Josh would practice walking by himself with no assistive device. After warming his body up with some arm exercises, Josh began to prepare for his walk. With hands clenched into fists to help him balance, he started forward, his gait still a bit awkward as his body continued to relearn the movements.

Kim strolled alongside Josh as he moved forward, keeping one hand on his safety belt. Another therapist followed behind him with his wheelchair.

"Do you need to take a break?" Kim asked after Josh paused for a brief second.

"Nope. Let's keep going," Josh replied with a determined look on his face.

Despite his resolute attitude, he quickly became fatigued after walking a few more steps, and had to sit down in his wheelchair. He would practice walking like this during every session, pushing himself to go just a little bit farther each time.

While the amount of progress Josh was making in such a short time was staggering, so were the volumes of pain he had to endure in the aftermath. The days following therapy were the most intense. He had grown accustomed to the muscle pain from his workouts: it was the nerve pain that caused him the most grief. As he'd sit in his chair with his leg rest propped up, I'd watch his legs hop around uncontrollably. The only thing that brought relief from this aggravation was the pain medicine his clinical doctor had prescribed when he was discharged from the hospital. Unfortunately, the same doctor was requesting Josh begin to wean himself from this medicine because of its potentially addictive side effects.

Because his legs remained so weak and his range of motion limited, Josh had to be careful while he was home alone during the day. He could stand up and move between his bed and his chair with the use of his walker, but he was still unable to stretch his midsection or bend his knees down to reach things. Each morning, I prepared meals that would be easy for him to put together and carry from the kitchen using his walker. Likewise, I had to make sure that any other personal items he would need during the day were placed in an accessible area while he was at home by himself.

I worried relentlessly about him. I worried that he would fall down and not be able to get back up, or not be able to reach his cell phone to call me if he did. I worried about his fragile emotional state, which always seemed to be on the verge of yet another setback. I worried about my mother-in-law trying to get him back and forth to therapy appointments in the ice and snow. All these worries were completely outside the realm of my control, yet I still succumbed to their unrelenting fears.

We both battled between apprehension that something would happen to hinder Josh's progress, and the amazing joy we felt as we watched him heal. Sharing our story with others and talking through each trial with close friends and family helped us overcome the darker moments. Our honesty wasn't a search for sympathy or a pat on the shoulder, but a chance to let those who might also be struggling against the unknown know that there was hope. We fought against the loneliness of our situation by encouraging others.

It was during that time when I heard the gentle voice of God whispering to me yet again. With Josh's approval, I began journaling some of our stories and posting them on an Internet blog called "Reflections from Room 908." After receiving positive feedback from others regarding the blog and the stories I was sharing, I then felt prompted to extend my online encouragement ministry even further. I created the Facebook page "Room 908 Ministries" and began sharing inspirational stories and Bible scriptures with my friends and family.

I could have used any number or name to describe my ministry, but I believed God was calling me to use Room 908 because it was where our story originated. It was the place where my husband lay fighting for his life in silence and pain; where the light of day was shut out and fear overshadowed every conversation. It was there I would stand next to Josh's bedside for hours, holding his head as the pain swelled. In that room, I had never felt so alone, yet surrounded by the presence of God in my life.

In reality, Room 908 was more than just four walls. It was a representation of the faithfulness of God in action and a reminder of His promises to us. It was a declaration that no matter what happened we would never be alone.

It had been seven long months since that fateful day in July, and getting to this point hadn't been easy. There had been so much emotional, physical, and psychological pain along the way. Yet despite the weight of that immense pressure, our family remained intact. Josh's body was healing, our relationships were healing, and our hearts were finally starting to mend.

God wasn't quite finished with us yet.

The next few weeks passed by too quickly, and we tried not to dwell on the fact that Josh's therapy was going to end soon. For weeks after he came home from the hospital, all he could focus on was returning to his therapy workouts, and his rapid rate of healing had been exhilarating. Now, none of us wanted the therapy to end. Pulling into the hospital entrance on Josh's last day, my heart was heavy.

"I can't believe this is my last day," Josh murmured as I pushed the elevator button for the second floor.

"Me either," I replied. Neither of us wanted to talk about the loneliness Josh would once again experience after today. Thankfully, Kim met us with a smile at the doorway of the workout room.

"Let's complete your exit interview and then we can get you ready for your big walk." Her enthusiasm encouraged our dampened moods.

After our exit interview, Josh chose to begin his session by doing some arm- and leg-strengthening exercises to warm up his body for the main event. Today he would walk the entire length of the longest hallway, using only his cane for support and with no breaks in between. His ability to sustain walking like this would help determine how well he would be able to mimic this in the real world, outside the hospital walls.

As Josh and his therapists prepared for his walk, I took a moment to reflect back over the events of the past eight months. It was overwhelming to think back to where we had begun and to see him standing up in front of me, getting ready to walk. So much had happened in such a relatively short span of time.

For a month, he had been lost to us, drifting in and out of a cloud of pain. Guillain-Barré had ascended upward in his body, slowly paralyzing him. Making its way toward his chest, it next compromised his lungs, and Josh was transferred to intensive care. After several weeks of waiting and uncertainty, the doctors were finally able to diagnose what was happening and a new future for us was unveiled.

The next two months were spent transitioning from the main hospital to the rehabilitation unit, in hopes that the nerves in Josh's body would finally wake up and he could begin his recovery. More pain, fear, and uncertainty awaited us as his nerves fired back to life and his lower body started functioning once again. There were the highs and lows of his inpatient therapy sessions. He would physically give every ounce of strength he had to push his body back, yet he was faced with disappointment when he had to deal with the side effects of that very same therapy.

There was the unbridled joy of knowing that he would be able to return home and our lives together could begin anew, coupled with the corresponding anxiety of what that life would actually be like. There was the emotional roller-coaster day of his discharge; leaving the nurses and therapists Josh had grown close to during the journey, and the celebrations of coming home. There were the weeks of transitions as I became Josh's primary caregiver and we began to adapt to our new way of living with a disability.

Finally, there was the joy of healing in earnest as his bedsore closed up and we were informed that he could begin attending outpatient therapy sessions. A whole new world had been unveiled to us as he advanced from his wheelchair to the parallel bars, to a walker, and finally standing up straight using only a cane for support. A whirlwind of emotions and circumstances had brought us to the current day.

It was hard for me to keep the tears at bay while I followed slowly behind Josh as he began his stroll down the long hallway. Holding my phone in front of me, I recorded every step he took. I marveled at how his gait had become less wobbly and his footing more secure. He was able to stand up straighter and hold his head high while he walked, instead of focusing on the ground and worrying about his feet. I couldn't wait to share the video with friends, family members, and coworkers who had been following our story and praying for us along the way.

When he was done with his walk, we made our way back to the workout room to say our final good-byes to Kim, her assistant, Bryce, and the other therapists who had been there for every step of Josh's outpatient therapy. We exchanged hugs, well wishes, and a few tears as we prepared to leave. I took one last picture of Josh standing between Kim and Bryce. This picture would become a precious keepsake for us; representing a time where healing and renewal thrived. We would never forget how their encouragement and support helped not only Josh's body to be restored, but our family as well.

The next morning during my quiet time after breakfast, I opened my Bible to the story of Jesus ascending into heaven as told by the Apostle Matthew. I had chosen to reflect on this particular event because it spoke about a major transition in the lives of Jesus's disciples. After the death, burial, and resurrection of Jesus, the lives of these eleven men would never be the same. They would face extremely difficult circumstances, yet Jesus promised he would provide them the strength to endure. He also promised they would never be alone.

Jesus was a man of his word.

> *"And surely I am with you always,*
> *to the very end of the age."*

Matthew 28:20

The conversation hummed in excited tones as the group of eleven men walked alongside Jesus, traveling to their intended destination. The last few days had brought with them events that none of them could have predicted. Their eyes were opened as Jesus explained everything had occurred as the fulfillment of scripture. It was all part of God's plan from the beginning.

They watched while Judas betrayed Jesus and the guards arrested him. They stood in the back of the room, listening to the crowd begging for his death. They saw the blood running down his back as he was brutally beaten by the Roman soldiers. They followed along with the crowd, witnessing Jesus struggling up the hill toward the place where he would be crucified, forced to carry his own cross. They comforted Jesus's mother, Mary, while her son's life slowly drained away. They saw the noonday sun turn to darkness for three hours and heard the voice of Jesus cry out as he breathed his last breath.

"Father, into your hands I commit my spirit!"

Their Savior was gone. Criminals punished with death by crucifixion were normally buried in unmarked graves, but Jesus wasn't a criminal, and nothing about his death was normal. Joseph of Arimathea, a wealthy member of the Sanhedrin Council, had personally requested that Pilate release Jesus's body to him after his death. He willingly relinquished his own burial tomb so that Jesus could be laid to rest privately and safely.

The disciples witnessed the massive stone rolled over the door to the burial chamber, sealing the body of their beloved for eternity. They wept bitterly, unable to understand why Jesus didn't intervene and prevent this from happening. Surely, with the lift of a finger, he could have called down a thousand angels from heaven to protect him from those who desired his death. His ministry was only starting to sink roots in their community and prosper.

Why did he have to die?

What were they going to do?

All those fears had vanished as they realized their Savior had conquered death and risen from the grave as the scriptures had prophesied. God's promise had been fulfilled. Jesus was the Messiah who would save the world from their sins, and the disciples were the witnesses who would spread this good news. They traveled down the road toward the village of Bethany with hearts full of unspeakable joy. They listened intently, hanging on every word that Jesus spoke about what their role would be in this new future. He promised they would be provided with the power and strength required to accomplish great works for the kingdom of God.

With heads and hearts still spinning in amazement, they were surprised to see Jesus suddenly stop walking and lift his hands up in the air. He began to pray encouragement over each one of them, smiling fondly at the group of men who would carry his gospel to the very ends of the earth. He blessed their ministries and he blessed their faithfulness.

Then, as suddenly as he had appeared to them in the upper room, he was gone. The clouds parted and Jesus ascended up into heaven. The disciples wouldn't see him again in this life, and the weight of their commission began to sink heavily onto their hearts. They breathed in the last words Jesus had spoken before he ascended as though their lives depended upon them.

"And surely I am with you always, to the very end of the age."

Josh, Jesi, and I were standing in the doorway of yet another major transition in our lives. Josh's outpatient therapy was now complete; his recovery wasn't. There was still so much for him to conquer. Like the disciples who had just received their great commission, we stood on the threshold of a new beginning, clinging to the promises given to us by Jesus.

From the very first, he had wrapped us into his loving arms and promised he would never let go. He had been there through the storms, as the wind and rain barraged us from all sides. He was there during times of fear and uncertainty. He sat beside us in the intensive care unit when we feared the worst. He never left as we battled through the physical and emotional pain of healing nerves. He celebrated with us as Josh was discharged from the hospital and returned home. He smiled as we rejoiced during every session of physical therapy watching the incredible rate of Josh's progress.

Our path had been littered with fears, disappointments and heartache, yet somehow we had navigated around each obstacle. It hadn't been easy. It had been messy and uncertain and had threatened to tear our family apart. There were times when we felt the weight of our burdens were too immense to bear, yet we were provided with the strength to endure.

Letting faith guide us through one day at a time, we learned to be patient and to rely on God.

Then, when the timing was just as He had planned all along, God gently reminded us that this wasn't the end. He had plans for our future. It was time for us to take our mat and go home.

Looking Back

Josh's Perspective

My advice to anyone diagnosed with Guillain-Barré syndrome, or any variation of neuromuscular disease, is to have lots and lots of patience. Nothing happens overnight. The healing is a slow, gradual process. The amount of pain involved is tough to deal with, but you have to mentally push through it, even when it hurts every single day. To a certain extent, you get used to the pain and it actually feels odd when it finally goes away.

Every person who goes through this is different, and there are no specific timetables for the recovery process. Initially we thought everything would be back to normal for us within six months to a year. It was difficult to watch that one-year mark pass, then two years, and now three years since my original diagnosis. Nothing really happened the way we thought it would.

I was very fortunate to have such an amazing group of people to help me through this. I was completely dependent upon others for the first few months after I came home. I'm not sure how I could have endured without the help from my parents, my physical therapists, my friends, and most especially, my wife. Maggie was my rock. Her unwavering belief in my abilities, her faith in God, and her unconditional love for me became my strength during those times I felt weak, useless, and afraid. I wouldn't be where I am today without her.

My mom was also a huge part of my recovery. She encouraged me and pushed me through the darker days when I struggled with loneliness. She transported me back and forth to my therapy sessions and helped pick up Jesi from school. Her support meant the world to me.

This whole experience definitely gave me a different perspective about faith and trusting in God. I found myself praying all the time; for myself and for my family. I needed help and because there was no running away, figuratively or literally, I just had to pray. What I saw as the biggest miracle of my situation was that my legs could come back from being paralyzed. While I won't be running marathons anytime soon, I can stand up and walk.

That, to me, is simply amazing.

EPILOGUE

Summer 2016

Now here we are, three years later. So much has happened since Josh completed his outpatient therapy. Our lives have become a journey of "firsts": the first family camping trip, the first full walk around the block, the first fishing excursion, the first lawn-mowing experience, and on and on. A thousand tiny moments bloomed into a garden of spectacular accomplishments. Each day brought with it a little more freedom than the last.

By the time Jesi began first grade in August 2014, Josh was able to drive his truck and pick her up from school every day. These bonding experiences would help seal their relationship back together. That same year, we began the process of applying for Social Security disability benefits to help us supplement some of our lost income. God was faithful yet again as we received a quick approval, apparently an uncommon occurrence for most first-time disability requests. These benefits would last for almost two years during the time we needed them the most.

The doctor visits that were so frequent in the beginning have now tapered off to only the occasional checkup. Josh's healing has continued its slow progress. He can walk around the

EPILOGUE

grocery store without becoming fatigued, drive long distances, stand up while fishing, and just recently was finally able to get into his kayak. Balance for him remains a challenge, and there are still movements he is limited in performing, such as bending down or carrying large objects. As we have learned throughout this entire journey, only faith and lots of patience will determine when his nerves will completely heal.

I have learned so much about myself, my own strengths and weaknesses, and how much my faith and belief in God truly defines who I am as a person during this season of my life. Emotionally, I still have moments where I struggle with the uncertainties of what the future will hold, but spiritually, I have located a sense of peace and understanding that I don't have to know all the answers. I believe in hope. I believe in miracles. Most of all, I believe in the amazing grace, mercy, and love of Jesus Christ, my Savior and Redeemer.

A new season is now on the horizon for us: the possibility of Josh returning to work. At face value, it seems a daunting and fearful impossibility, especially with the challenges he's still physically faced with. However, we've learned to trust that no matter what happens, we will be provided for. God has a plan for our lives, for our future. The fact that you are reading this right now is a perfect example of that truth.

My intention in writing *Take Your Mat and Go Home* was to share this hope with you. I pray that you have found encouragement and inspiration within the pages of this book. I pray that you will lean on the promises displayed in our story when you find your own world rocked by an unforeseen or unexpected situation. Never be afraid to cry out to God. He hears every prayer and every cry of your heart, and He will never abandon or forsake you.

God is faithful. You will see.

ABOUT THE AUTHOR

Raised in the small farming community of Lamar, Missouri, she chose to remain close to home after graduating from high school. Attending Southwest Missouri State University (now known as Missouri State University), located in Springfield, Missouri, Maggie graduated in 2000 with a Bachelor's degree in Accounting. After college, she worked eight years in the Accounting department for Willow Brook Foods, a local turkey processing company. When Willow Brook was purchased by Cargill Meat Solutions in 2008, Maggie began her accounting work with Hamra Enterprises.

After her husband's illness in the summer of 2013, Maggie turned to writing as a means of personal therapy. She began journaling her stories and sharing them in online blogs and on social media. She discovered that her writing was helping to encourage others dealing with difficult situations in their own lives. This revelation soon brought life to *Take Your Mat and Go Home*, her first published work.

Maggie lives in southwest Missouri with her husband Josh and their daughter Jesi. She continues to share her personal stories of encouragement with her Room 908 Facebook Ministry. You can find out more about Room 908 and Maggie and Josh's journey with Guillain-Barre at www.maggieballen.com.

ACKNOWLEDGMENTS

I can't say thank you enough to everyone who has played a part, big or small, in the creation of this book; from the very beginning of Josh's illness to the Kickstarter supporters who were pivotal in helping the book get published.

To Nancy Hughes, thank you for your wisdom, words of advice, and mentoring, during the writing and publishing process. Your support and prayers have meant the world to me.

To Debra Samek, thank you for accepting the responsibility of becoming my writing accountability partner, helping gives names to each chapter and deciding on the title. This would not have been possible without your shoulder to lean on.

To both Josh's parents and mine, the love and support you have given to us all of our lives is beyond words. Neither of us could be where we are right now without you.

To Robin and Amy, my sweet cousins-in-law and sisters in Christ, your friendship and love brought me through some of the darkest days of Josh's illness and the new reality we faced when he came home from the hospital. You are both precious to me.

To my co-workers at Hamra Enterprises, thank you for allowing me the time I needed to be with Josh when he needed me the most and for the continued support of our family.

To all of our dedicated "prayer warriors," please know that your prayers have supported Josh, Jesi, and me through days where it didn't seem we would make it through to the other side.

To Josh's physical therapists both during his time in the hospital and during his outpatient therapy, your encouragement and positive attitudes enabled Josh to push through the pain and learn how to walk again. Josh's time in therapy has created priceless memories that will never be forgotten.

None of this would have been possible had it not been for my faith and the Holy Spirit who guided my words. All glory, praise, and honor goes to Him who led us through our storm.

To my husband, Josh, who likes to joke that if he hadn't got sick there would be no book, thank you for your unending patience with me during my writing journey. Thank you for allowing me to share our story and for supporting me every step of the way. I love you with all of my heart.